Second Edition

Cambridge Primary Path 5

CAMBRIDGE

Activity Book
with Digital Pack

Niki Joseph

1 How can we make a difference?

1 ▶ 1.1 **Watch the video. Complete the graphic organizer.**

> By cleaning up her local beach   ~~Dr. Jane Tam, International Doctors~~
> By helping sick people and preventing diseases
> Mae Powell, Green Team conservation club   By inspiring people to play sports
> Mark Jackson, volunteer wheelchair basketball coach

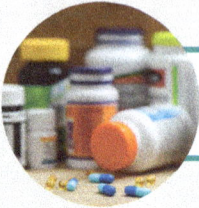

Who? Dr. Jane Tam, International Doctors **How?** _____

Who? _____ **How?** _____

Who? _____ **How?** _____

2 Key Words 1 **Choose the correct words to complete the sentences.**

> conservation   disease   environment   inspire
> society   talent   vaccination   volunteers

a You have a v_____ so that you don't get a d_____.

b People who give their time for free are v_____.

c There are many c_____ groups that work to protect the e_____.

d Everyone has a special t_____. What is yours?

e Some people i_____ us and make us want to do things better.

f Many people want to make a difference in s_____.

Ready to Read: Nonfiction

1 **Key Words 2** **Match the sentence halves.**

1 A developer
2 An innovation
3 When you code a computer
4 Computers, tablets, and smart phones
5 An ambassador
6 When you get paid for doing a job or a sport,

a you give it instructions.
b creates new things, for example, new phone apps.
c is a new way of doing something.
d represents an organization or a country.
e you are a professional.
f are all electronic.

2 **Choose the correct words to complete the sentences.**

> invent   reacts   successful   skill

a Deepika's photocatalyst _____ with sunlight.

b Let's _____ something to take the salt out of seawater.

c That girl is a very _____ tennis player—she wins every competition!

d What can you do well? What is your special _____?

3 **Find and circle 10 words that you have learned.**

> developer   professional
> electronic   skill
> successful   invent
> react   innovation
> ambassador   code

s	u	c	c	e	s	s	f	u	l	b	k	u
a	d	v	f	x	z	b	i	q	h	f	s	q
q	r	e	a	c	t	m	n	d	h	p	e	r
l	w	l	e	o	t	t	v	y	u	c	v	y
j	h	e	i	d	e	v	e	l	o	p	e	r
o	j	c	x	e	g	l	n	x	w	g	y	h
i	a	t	v	m	k	q	t	c	z	h	p	m
s	p	r	a	m	b	a	s	s	a	d	o	r
k	z	o	b	n	l	g	j	f	w	m	k	a
i	n	n	o	v	a	t	i	o	n	a	o	i
l	s	i	c	e	r	h	d	f	c	h	d	s
l	x	c	v	y	u	p	w	s	s	z	m	p
p	r	o	f	e	s	s	i	o	n	a	l	j

Reading Strategy: Asking Questions

Asking questions about a text helps you to understand and remember it. You can think of questions to ask before, during, and after reading a text.

1 Look at the photo and the title of the article. Why do you think the girl is sitting alone? Mark ✓.

She doesn't want to talk. ☐   She doesn't have any friends. ☐   She's waiting for her friends. ☐

2 Read the text and answer the questions.

a   Who is Natalie Hampton? _____

b   What has she invented? _____

c   Why did she do that? _____

Where Can I Sit?

Is lunchtime at school frightening? Do you worry about where to sit? Natalie Hampton used to worry every day. Then, she developed an app to help people who, like her, often sat alone at lunchtime. This is her story!

It began with the words, "You can't sit with us." One day Natalie wanted to sit with some classmates at lunchtime, but they were mean and unfriendly and wouldn't let her. Every day was the same. She had no friends, and she always had to sit by herself. Natalie became sad, anxious, and unhappy. In the end, she talked to her parents, and they decided that she should change schools.

On Natalie's first day at her new school, a complete stranger asked her, "Do you need help?" That question changed her life. It was the first time that someone at school had spoken kindly to her for a very long time. Later, that girl became one of Natalie's best friends. Natalie started to enjoy school. She made new friends, and she felt happy.

Every day she had lunch with her new friends, but, from the first day, she noticed a girl who always ate lunch alone. Natalie knew exactly what that felt like, so one day she invited the girl to join her for lunch. That girl also became one of her best friends.

Natalie decided to do something more. She invented an app. It's called Sit with Us, and it tells you about lunch tables where people will welcome you. Here's how it works. You download and install the app onto your cell phone, and then you can find "open lunches." An open lunch means that there is a table where you can sit and where people will talk to you. It all happens on your cell phone, so it's private. No one will say, "You can't sit with us."

You can also become a Sit with Us ambassador. You take the Ambassador's Pledge and promise to be kind to everyone, especially people on their own. Then, you can invite students to join you at your own "open lunch" event. By developing this app, Natalie has changed many people's lives.

3 **Circle the correct answer.**

a   Natalie changed schools because **her parents moved** / **she was unhappy**.

b   A complete stranger **offered to help her** / **was mean to her**.

c   Natalie **made** / **downloaded** an app.

d   The app tells you where there are **tables where no one is sitting** / **open lunches**.

e   An ambassador has to make **a wish** / **a promise**.

f   Natalie has changed **a few** / **a lot of** people's lives.

4 **Here are some ideas for the Ambassador's Pledge. Can you add more ideas?**

be friendly to people   talk to new people in a nice way

_____

_____

_____

_____

Hi! Welcome to my open lunch!

5 **Do you think the _Sit with Us_ app is a good idea? Why/Why not?**

_____

_____

_____

Grammar in Context

Quantifiers

We use quantifiers to talk about amounts.

All the children sat at the tables.
Most children brought lunch from home.
Some charities are international.

A few volunteers work on Saturdays.
No houses had electricity.

1 **Match the underlined quantifiers with the words that have the same meaning.**

1 I'd like <u>some</u> batteries, please.
2 <u>All</u> the children wanted to take part in the charity event.
3 I have <u>a few</u> ideas, but not many.
4 <u>Most</u> people didn't understand the invention.
5 We have <u>no</u> fruit to eat.

a none
b lots
c two or three
d one or two
e everyone

2 **Write the words in the correct order.**

a our / to / few / gave / A / people / money / charity

A few people gave money to our charity.

b volunteers / Most / work / their / enjoy

_____

c to travel / car / Some / by / people / like

_____

d germs / water / this / There / no / are / in

_____

e children / enjoy / classes / the / the / All

_____

3 **Circle the correct words to complete the sentences.**

a **All / Some** children joined the Conservation Club, and others joined the Art Club.
b **All / A few** people are good at recycling, but many people are not.
c **A few / All** doctors can vaccinate against diseases.
d **No / Some** developers have invented an app that will do my homework yet!
e **Most / A few** people have a special talent, but perhaps you don't know what yours is!
f There are **some / most** drinking fountains around the school.

4 **Complete the sentences using *some*, *all*, *most*, *a few*, or *no*.**

a I bought this canvas recently—only ___a few___ days ago, I think.

b _____ the batteries in our home can be charged with sunlight.
We don't have to buy batteries anymore.

c At the exhibition, _____ people just wanted to look at the paintings.
Only 1% of the people who came actually bought anything.

d I have _____ plans for the weekend. There's nothing in my calendar.
What are you doing? Should we go to the beach?

e It's really hard to get into that school. Only _____ kids are successful.

5 **Look at the picture. Write sentences using these phrases and the quantifiers *most*, *some*, *all*, *a few*, or *no*.**

> sitting at tables   eating school lunches
> eating their food   drinking water   eating sandwiches

_____

_____

_____

_____

_____

My Life

Complete these sentences so that they are true for you.

All my _____.

Only a few of _____.

I have some _____.

No _____.

Most _____.

Spelling Patterns and Word Study

1 Look at the pictures and mark ✓ the words with the same sound as *niece*.

 **a**
 **b**
 **c**
 **d**

ceiling ☐   eight ☐   field ☐   beige ☐

2 Write the words in the correct row according to the sound.

believe   brief   eighty   neighbor   receipt   weigh

niece	
rein	

Oracy

1 Which Oracy Time! topic did your group discuss? Mark ✓.

> **Oracy Time!**
>
> You should always tell the truth. ☐
> Talking is more important than listening. ☐

I'm Liam.

2 Did you agree or disagree with the Oracy Time! topic? Why?

I agreed because _____

_____ .

I disagreed because _____

_____ .

I'm Emma.

3 Which ground rule is the most difficult for you to use or follow? Why?

I think _____ is the most difficult ground rule to use or follow

because _____ .

Parentheses

We use parentheses to add extra information to a sentence or to explain the meaning of something. There are always two parentheses ( ).

1 **Add the missing parentheses.**

a WWF the World Wildlife Fund is also known as the World Wide Fund for Nature.

b The bus will pick the children up or their parents can take them to school.

c I want to donate some money to the ASPCA the American Society for the Prevention of Cruelty to Animals.

d You can do your homework now or you can do it at home.

e We're organizing a three-hour workshop juice and cookies included on Saturday, January 20.

f My sister goes to QES Queen Elizabeth School.

g The doctor a specialist in children's diseases took care of my cousins after the fire.

h The twins 10 years old spent three hours playing computer games last night.

2 **Match each picture with one of the sentences in Activity I.**

①

②

③

3 **Do you know any organizations with initials for their names? What do the initials stand for? Write sentences that explain the initials. Use parentheses.**

a _____

b _____

c _____

Writing

1 READ Read the letter on page 15 in the Student's Book. Answer the questions.

a Who is the letter to? _____

b What is the event? _____

c Why are the students organizing it? _____

d What is KIDS? _____

_____

e What do the students want people to do? _____

_____

2 PLAN You are going to write a letter to friends and neighbors about an event to raise funds for a charity. Choose a charity. Think of an event. Make notes in the graphic organizer.

About the Event

About the Charity

How Can People Help?

Event Details (Date, Time, Place)

3 WRITE Use your notes to write your letter. Remember to start and end correctly.

4 EDIT Read your work and mark ✓.

Did you:

- include a greeting and closing? ☐
- include practical information about the event? ☐
- try to persuade your readers? ☐
- use parentheses? ☐

1 | Key Words 4 | **Complete the sentences with the correct form of the words.**

> announcement   curious   get lost   hang out with   interrupt   realize

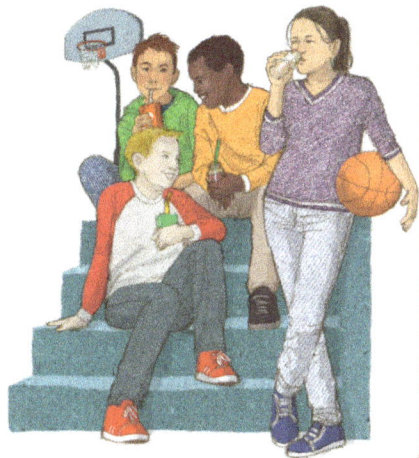

a I love _____ my friends on the weekend.

b Young animals are often really _____. They spend a lot of time exploring new things.

c Did you read the _____ on the website? Our art teacher is leaving at the end of the year.

d I don't like the first day at a new school because I always _____.

e I was looking for the math classroom. But when I heard music, I _____ I was in the wrong place.

f I hate it when I'm talking and someone _____. It's so rude.

2 **Match the words with the definitions.**

1 ignore

2 offer

3 weird

4 immediately

5 obviously

6 introduce

a when you tell someone another person's name when they meet for the first time

b strange, odd

c when you ask someone if they would like something

d now

e when you don't talk, listen, or pay attention to someone

f in a way that is easy to see or understand

Hannah, this is Eduardo.

Hi, Eduardo!

1 **Read the story. Put the pictures in the correct order.**

Lou and her older brother Jack were bored, so they decided to walk home from school a different way. They didn't immediately notice that Mrs. Belfour had come out of her front door because they were too busy looking at the seven little puppies running and playing in her front yard.

"Oh, hello, Mrs. Belfour," they both said when they noticed her standing on her front porch.

"Hello, Lou and Jack. Look at all these puppies! My dog had them a month ago!"

Lou said, "They're very cute."

"Do you think so?" asked Mrs. Belfour. "Hmm. Would your family like to adopt one when they are old enough to leave their mother?"

"Really? We'll have to ask our mom and dad first …" Jack said.

"But I know they will say yes!" Lou interrupted.

"That would be wonderful," said Mrs. Belfour. "I'll still need to find homes for the others, though. I don't know how I'm going to do that. There are too many puppies for me to keep all of them. Obviously, taking care of that many dogs is a lot of work!"

Jack said, "We'll ask our parents about adopting one, Mrs. Belfour. But I don't think they'll let

us have more. Come on, Lou, let's go see what they say!"

As soon as they got home, they asked their mom. She said she'd be happy to adopt one puppy, and their dad agreed when he came home that evening.

"Poor Mrs. Belfour," their mom said, "I hope she can find homes for all those puppies!"

Lou had a weird look on her face, like she was thinking about something funny. "I have an idea, Mom!"

The next day, Jack and Lou went to school dressed up as dogs! They told their classmates about Mrs. Belfour's puppies. "She needs to find homes for six of them. Do you know anyone who'd like to adopt a puppy?" By noon, some of the teachers knew about the puppies, too, and the principal made an announcement to the entire school.

Over the next few weeks, a lot of Jack's and Lou's classmates went to Mrs. Belfour's house to see the puppies. Not only were all the puppies adopted, but Mrs. Belfour was introduced to the children's parents. And Jack and Lou continued to visit Mrs. Belfour, too. They even took their puppy, Biscuits, with them so that it could hang out with its mom!

Explore the Text

Reading Strategy: Cause and Effect

A cause is the reason something happens. The effect is what happens because of this cause. A cause can have more than one effect.

2 **Match the causes and effects. Remember the order of events.**

Causes

1 Lou and Jack were bored,

2 They walked home a different way,

3 Lou said the puppies were cute,

4 Their mom hoped Mrs. Belfour could find homes for all the puppies,

5 Lou had an idea,

6 They told their classmates about the puppies,

7 Lou and Jack took their puppy, Biscuits, to Mrs. Belfour's house,

Effects

a so they saw the puppies in Mrs. Belfour's yard.

b so some of their classmates adopted them.

c so it could hang out with its mother.

d so they walked home a different way.

e so she and Jack went to school dressed as dogs

f so Mrs. Belfour asked if they'd like to adopt one.

g so Lou thought of a way to help get the puppies adopted.

3 **Read the questions and circle the correct answers.**

1 Why did Lou and Jack go to school dressed as dogs?
   a It was a dress-up day.
   b They wanted people to listen to them.
   c They love dogs.

2 What did some of the children in the school do?
   a They dressed up as dogs.
   b They made an announcement to the whole school.
   c They adopted the puppies.

3 Mrs. Belfour found homes for
   a all the puppies and the mother dog.
   b the mother dog and some of the puppies.
   c all the puppies.

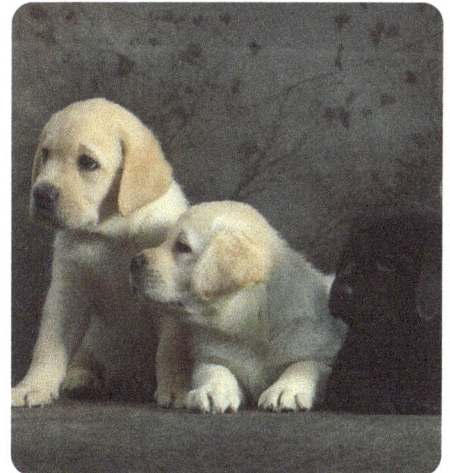

4 **What do you think is the best title for the story? Mark ✓.**

Lou and Jack Take a New Way Home ☐

Happy Dogs ☐

Lou and Jack Help Out! ☐

Grammar in Context

Causative Verbs: *have something done*

We use causative verbs to describe actions that we ask someone else to do for us. We use *have* and the past participle of the verb.

Marcia had her hair cut. (This sentence doesn't tell us who cut Marcia's hair.)

1 Match the sentence halves.

1 She has all her meals   a   polished once a week.
2 She has her nails   b   cooked for her.
3 She has her emails   c   washed every day.
4 She has her hair   d   read to her.

2 Write the words in the correct order.

a cleaned / her / has / house / The rich lady / every day

_____

b cell phone / had / fixed / my / I

_____

c cut / month / has / hair / every / Mom / her

_____

d last year / painted / house / their / had / Our neighbors

_____

3 Someone did these things for you!

a Did your mom clean the windows herself?

No, she had them cleaned.

b Did you paint the house yourselves?

No, we _____

c Did you wash the clothes yourself?

No, I _____

d Did you cut your hair yourself?

No, I _____

e Did you take the photos yourselves?

No, we _____

4 Complete the sentences with the verbs in parentheses.

a My house was very dirty, so I (clean) _I had it cleaned._

b My yard was full of leaves, so I (clean) _____.

c My phone didn't work, so I (fixed) _____.

d My hair was long and messy, so I (cut and wash) _____.

5 Rewrite the sentences.

a Someone cuts the grass in their yard.

They _____.

b The window cleaners clean our windows every month.

We _____.

c The man in the store repaired my computer last week.

I _____.

d The photographer takes our photo every year.

We _____.

My Life

What did you or your family have done last month?

We _____.

I _____.

My brother/sister _____.

My mom _____.

1 Complete the table about respecting others with these phrases. Some can go in more than one place.

> not being mean to your classmates   not littering in the street   sitting still
> not playing very loud video games   keeping your yard clean   playing nicely
> listening to family members   putting your hand up before you speak

In the Classroom	On the Playground

At Home	In the Community

2 Add one more idea to each category.

3 Complete the sentences.

I respect my parents by _____

_____

I respect my friends by _____

_____

I respect my teachers by _____

_____

I respect the community by _____

_____

I respect the world by _____

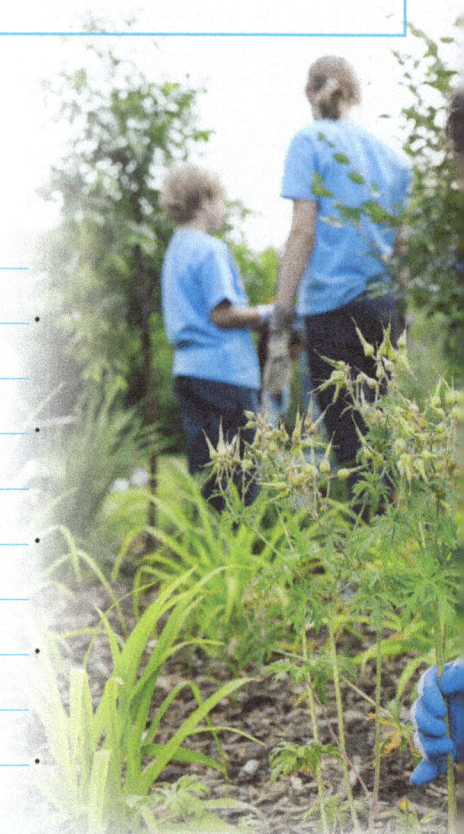

_____

Check Your Oracy: Ground Rules

1	My group followed the ground rules for discussion.	All the time / Most of the time / Sometimes
2	Were any ground rules broken? If so, which rules?	
3	Are there any ground rules you think need to be added or changed?	

The Big Challenge

How can we create a new community project?

a **What community project did you plan?**

b **How well did you do? Color the stars to give yourself a score.***

I researched the problems in my community.	☆☆☆☆☆
I worked with my classmates on planning our project.	☆☆☆☆☆
I practiced my presentation before I presented it.	☆☆☆☆☆
I gave my presentation to the class.	☆☆☆☆☆

*(5 = Awesome! 4 = Pretty good, 3 = OK, 2 = Could be better, 1 = Needs more work!)

c **Which other project did you like the best?**

d **What could you do better next time?**

The Big Question and Me

Because of the things I have learned in this unit,

I will

1 Choose the correct words to complete sentences.

> announcement   code   get lost   inspire   international   skills

a I'm learning languages because I want to work for an _____ company.

b Did you read the principal's _____? He's going to work in New Zealand next year.

c I'm going to speak more in class because I want to improve my speaking _____.

d Some people _____ us to try harder.

e I'm learning how to _____, and I understand more about websites and apps now.

f I always _____ in this shopping mall—it's so big!

2 Choose the correct words to complete the crossword.

> code   conservation   disease
> germs   ignore   interrupt
> society   talent
> volunteer   weird

Across

2 When you write computer programs, you _____.

3 When something is strange or unusual, it is _____.

8 Nature _____ means protecting wildlife.

9 When you get sick because you have an infection, you have a _____.

10 If you speak when someone else is speaking, you _____ them.

Down

1 Someone who works, but doesn't get paid is a _____.

4 When you don't listen to someone, you _____ them.

5 A _____ is a large group of people who live in the same country and have the same laws, traditions, etc.

6 If there are _____ in drinking water, you shouldn't drink it.

7 If you have a _____ for something, you are very good at it.

3 Look at the pictures. Write the words.

c _ _ _ _ _ _

g _ _ _ _ _ _ _ _

e _ _ _ _ _ _ _

4 Choose the correct quantifiers to complete the sentences.

all   most   some   a few   no

Tina   I'm so happy it's Thursday—nearly the weekend! What are you doing on Saturday?

Hayley   I don't know. I have ¹_____ plans.

Tina   ²_____ the volunteers are going to hang out at Emily's—like, everyone's going to be there! The whole class! Do you want to come?

Hayley   Sure! That sounds like fun!

Tina   Yeah, we're celebrating! ³_____ of us have completed our conservation tasks. ⁴_____ people, three or four, I think, haven't finished yet, though.

Hayley   I know, I think there are about five, including Steve and Maddie, who need to do some more work. But there are still ⁵_____ days to go. We have to finish by next Monday.

Tina   That's true and everyone can help them.

Hayley   Let's do that at Emily's!

Tina   That's a great idea! See you there!

5 Rewrite the sentences. Use causative verbs.

a   The man fixed my bike for me. I had my bike fixed._____

b   The painters painted my grandparents' house. My grandparents _____

_____.

c   The hair stylist cut my hair for me. I _____.

d   The store printed some photos. I _____.

e   Dad put up some bookshelves in my room. I _____

_____.

6 Add parentheses in the correct places.

a   The volunteers will meet you at 10 a.m. or you can drop in the day before.

b   SAHA Save a Horse Australia is a charity for horses.

c   The children who were very excited couldn't wait for summer vacation.

d   The ambulance which had its siren and lights on moved quickly through the traffic.

e   The teacher who was new at the school asked the children to find out about a charity.

SPEAKING MISSION

1 Match the words with the definitions.

1 donation   a when you collect money for a charity

2 fundraising   b promise

3 help out   c to achieve your goals

4 participate   d to take part

5 pledge   e an objective, or goal

6 sponsor   f to do something for someone

7 succeed   g money or things given to help an organization or people

8 target   h to give money to someone who is doing something to raise money for a charity

2 What does Carlos say to Dan? Put the dialogue in the correct order.

Dan   Hello, Carlos!

Carlos   1   c

Dan   Which charity are you supporting?

Carlos   2 _____

Dan   Yes, I would. It sounds good.
How much money do you want to raise?

Carlos   3 _____

Dan   What time does the walk start?

Carlos   4 _____

Dan   Cool! Where do we meet?

Carlos   5 _____

Dan   I know it. What do we need to bring?

Carlos   6 _____

a At 10 a.m.

b Bring some good walking shoes, a hat, and some water.

c Hi, would you like to join our fundraising event?

d It's an international charity. It's called FMN (Forgetmenot). It's for children in India, Nepal, and Uganda. Would you like to join us?

e Near the bridge in the center of town.

f We're not sure. We're going to do a walk, and we want people to sponsor us.

What can you remember about Unit 1? Do the quiz.

1 Which was not a question on page 6 in the Student's Book?

  a How can we help other people?

  b What can we do to help animals?

  c What can we do to improve our neighborhood?

2 Which person did you read about on page 9 of the Student's Book?

  a a girl who invented a way of making clean drinking water

  b a boy who created an app for babies

  c a female artist from New Zealand

3 How did Courtney "read people's minds" in the story on pages 18–21 in the Student's Book?

  a She was a really nice girl.

  b She could read things very quickly.

  c She looked at the people carefully.

4 When are ground rules important?

  a when we are working on our own

  b when we are working with others

  c when we are reading

5 Look at the picture. Write the word.

  _____

6 Choose the correct quantifier to complete the sentence.

  Help! What can I do? I don't know. I have _____ idea!

7 Which word do the underlined letters sound like? Circle *niece* or *rein*.

  a b<u>ei</u>ge   b n<u>ei</u>ghbor   c w<u>ei</u>gh   d <u>ei</u>ght

8 Look at the picture. Write the word.

  _____

9 Do we use parentheses to

  a end a letter?

  b make some information more important?

  c give extra information in a sentence?

10 Complete the sentence with the verb in parentheses.

  My Mom went to the hair stylist yesterday. She _____ her hair _____ (cut).

Check your answers in the Student's Book. How did you do?

8–10 ☐ Wow!   6–7 ☐ Good job!   0–5 ☐ Try harder!

? 😊 **How can we make a difference?** Write three things.

_____

_____

2 How can we make our dreams come true?

1 ▶ 2.1 **Watch the video. Complete the graphic organizer.**

> has to be creative   has to be in good shape   is a digital artist
> is in a training program   solves problems all day
> wants to be a video game designer   wants to design rollercoasters
> wants to play in the World Cup   was good at math in school

Making Their Dreams Come True

Cam Aromdee

Jo Mattis

Tyler Green

_____

2 Key Words 1 **Choose the correct words to complete the sentences.**

> ambition   college   dedicated   training program   degree   creative   career

a I want to be a famous singer. That's my _____ in life.

b Mackenzie is going to _____ next year to study nursing.

c My sister is very _____. She always makes the presents she gives.

d My brother got his _____ from Harvard.

e The tennis _____ is three weeks long.

f What do you need to study if you want a _____ as an engineer?

g If you want to be really good at something, you have to be _____.

1 **Key Words 2** Look at the pictures. Write the jobs.

sculptor   composer   veterinarian   instructor   astronaut

a   b   c   d   e

2 Choose the correct words to complete the crossword.

astronaut   biology   composer   emotion   inspiration   instructor
sculptor   specialize   undergraduate   veterinarian

Across

1   a person who makes sculptures
5   a doctor who works with sick animals
10   to spend time studying or learning about one subject

Down

2   a student studying for a degree
3   the scientific study of living things
4   someone or something that gives you ideas for doing something
6   a person who travels into space
7   someone who teaches a sport or activity
8   someone who writes music
9   a strong feeling, (e.g., love, anger)

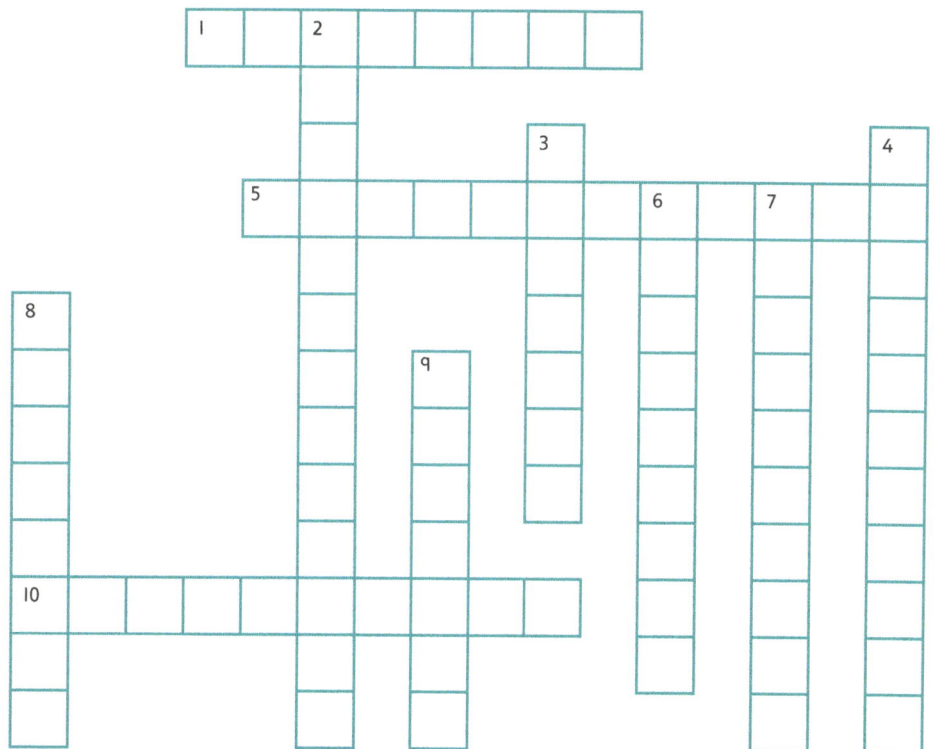

Reading Strategy: Author's Purpose

The author's purpose is the reason he/she wrote the text: to inform, persuade, or entertain.

1 **What is the main purpose of these texts? Complete the table. One can go in more than one place.**

story   textbook   advertisement   poem   encyclopedia   magazine article

To Inform	To Persuade	To Entertain

2 **Look at the text. What sort of text is it?** _____

Preparing for
the World of Work

Do you have a dream job? Would you like to be a professional soccer player? A brain surgeon? An astronaut?

Several weeks ago, the principal of a U.K. elementary school wrote to the students' parents about the school's World of Work Day. She invited students to come to school in the clothes they would wear for their dream job. She knew that a lot of them would choose to be celebrities (athletes, musicians, etc.), but very few people actually become celebrities. So, the teacher told parents that students could not come dressed as celebrities. Those students who had dreams of being professional athletes or entertainers had to dress up for different careers.

One of the parents sent the principal's letter to a national newspaper, and some people reacted badly to the teacher's idea. British athlete Jack Green, who competed in two Olympic Games, posted his thoughts on Twitter. He believes parents should not discourage their children. Every parent should support their child's dream, but they must also make sure the child understands that succeeding will be difficult.

But how difficult is it to be a successful athlete, brain surgeon, or composer? Some people might be born with natural talent, but, for other people, it takes a lot of hard work. One popular theory claimed a few years ago that it took 10,000 hours of practice to

become an expert at any skill. And this is true whatever your dream job might be: lawyer, engineer, architect, or ballet dancer. But how long is 10,000 hours? Imagine you want to be a professional soccer player. If you practice for two hours per day, for five days a week, how long would it take to get to 10,000 hours of practice? Well, after a year, you will have practiced about 500 hours. That would mean you had to practice for 20 years!

So, whatever your dream job is, if you're like most of us, you're going to have to work hard!

3 **Read the text. Why didn't the principal let the students come to school dressed as celebrities? Circle the correct answer.**

a because few people become celebrities

b because she thought dressing up as a celebrity would be difficult

c because celebrities don't work hard

4 **Read the text again and answer the questions. Circle the correct answers.**

1 What did the students wear on the World of Work Day?

a their parents' clothes

b the clothes of the job they want to do

c any sports clothes they had

2 What does Jack Green think?

a It's not difficult to become a professional athlete.

b Parents should support children's dreams.

c Education is more important than a good job.

3 What is the 10,000 hour theory?

a Professional athletes need to practice for 10,000 hours.

b A professional athlete's career lasts 10,000 hours.

c It takes 10,000 hours of practice to become an expert at any skill.

4 Why does the author show that it would take 20 years to reach 10,000 hours of practice if you practiced two hours per day?

a to show how long 10,000 hours is

b to show how easy becoming an expert is

c to show that only people with natural talent succeed

5 What is the author's purpose in writing this article?

a to inform

b to entertain

c to persuade

5 **What is your dream job? What skills will you need to become an expert at the job?**

_____

_____

_____

_____

Grammar in Context

Past Tense with *ago*

We use the past tense with *ago* to say how long before the present moment something happened. *Ago* is always used with a length of time.

Several weeks ago, the principal of a U.K. elementary school wrote to the parents …
One popular theory claimed a few years ago that it took 10,000 hours of practice …

1 These phrases can all be used with *ago*. Put them in order from the shortest to the longest length of time.

a month ☐   three days ☐   a couple of minutes [1]

two weeks ☐   a few years ☐   an hour ☐

2 Write the words in the correct order.

a a week / Maggie / my mom / ago / called

<u>Maggie called my mom a week ago.</u>

b We / ago / years / three / Brazil / visited

_____

c I / games / friends / ago, / video / my / An hour / was playing / with

_____

d A week / Tianna / this / ago, / was reading / book

_____

e fifteen / email / his / checked / man / The / ago / minutes

_____

3 Write questions with *you*. Then, answer the questions. Use *ago* if necessary.

1 **A** Have / ever / see / a whale ?

_____

B Yes, I _____ !
A When / see one?

_____

B I / see / one / a few months

_____

2 **A** Have / ever / visit / New York City?

_____

B Yes, I _____ !
A When / go?

_____

B I / go / there / six weeks

_____

4 **The story is in the wrong order! Read it and write the events in the correct order on the time line.**

Three days ago, he showed his new car to his best friend. A week ago, he drove his new car to the mountains. Two weeks and six days ago, he drove his new car to the supermarket. Yesterday, Mr. Fredericks took his daughter to school in his new car. Three weeks ago, Mr. Fredericks bought a new car.

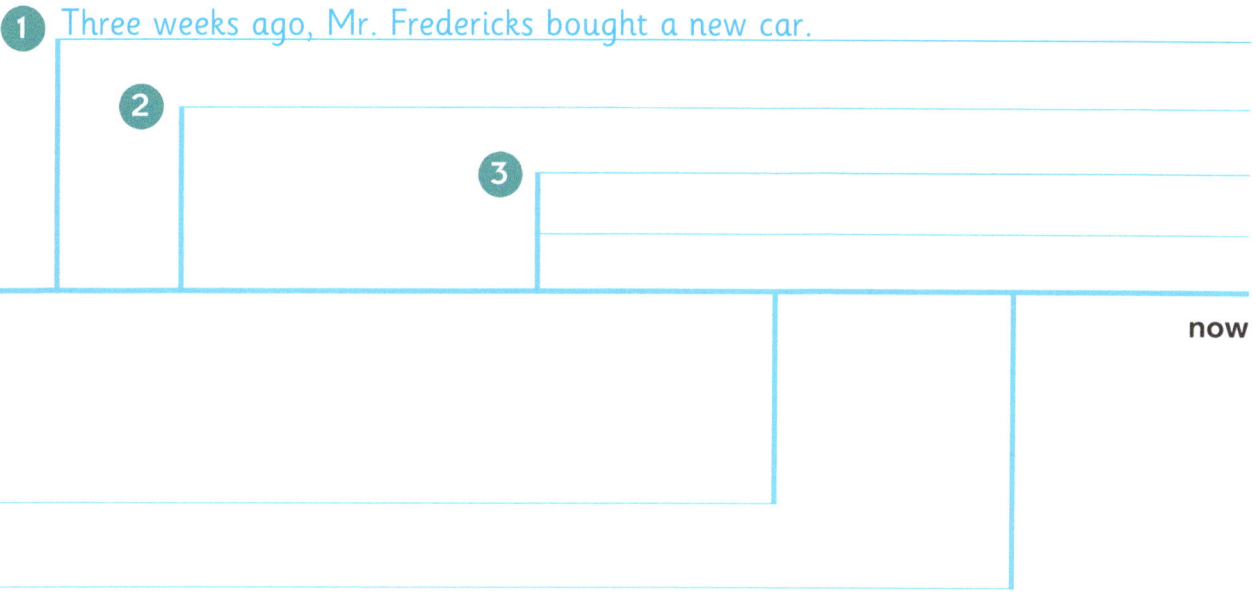

1 Three weeks ago, Mr. Fredericks bought a new car.

2 _____

3 _____

the past   now

4 _____

5 _____

5 **Complete the sentences with the past simple of the verbs in parentheses. Add *ago* if necessary.**

a Cathy _____ (design) her new website yesterday _____.

b The instructor _____ (explain) how to pass the ball quickly _____.

c We _____ (go) on a family vacation a year _____.

d My parents _____ (fly) to London two days _____.

e I _____ (see) your friend at the training program this morning _____.

f I _____ (meet) the scuba-diving instructor a couple of days _____.

My Life

Complete these sentences so that they are true for you.

An hour ago, I _____.

I _____ three days ago.

Six months ago, I _____.

27

Spelling Patterns and Word Study

1 Look at the pictures and write the words. They all have the same sound at the end.

f _____

p _____

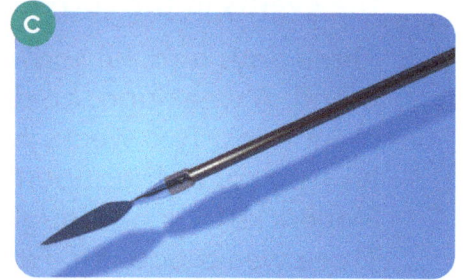

s _____

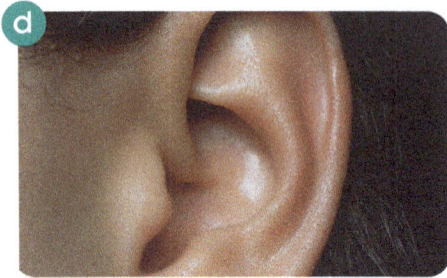

e _____

v _____

s _____

2 Complete the sentences with a word ending in *-eer*, *-ier*, *-ere*, or *-ear*.

a My mom has a good c _____ in banking.

b Next y _____, my family and I are going on vacation in the U.S.A.

c Our school is n _____ the center of town.

d This isn't your business! Don't i _____!

e H _____ you are! This is your book, isn't it?

f I like this bank. The c _____ is really friendly.

Oracy

1 Which Oracy Time! topic did you and your partner talk about the most? Mark ✓.

2 Write three probing questions that you asked or heard.

⭐ **Oracy Time!**

In school, we should only study the subjects we like. ☐

Kids have more fun than adults. ☐

_____

_____

_____

Adjectives with Prepositions

Some adjectives are followed by prepositions.
Remember the prepositions that follow these adjectives:

good at   **interested** in   **bored** with

1 **Read the sentences and write the missing prepositions.**

a My dad is good _____ learning new languages.

b Some people are interested _____ how we show our emotions.

c I get bored _____ video games really easily.

d What are you good _____ ?

e The children were interested _____ finding out more about music.

f We never get bored _____ going to the beach.

2 **Write full sentences to answer these questions for yourself. Say why!**

What are you good at?

a I'm good _____ because _____ .

What are you interested in?

b I'm interested _____ because _____ .

What are you never bored with?

c I'm never bored _____ because _____ .

Writing

1 READ Look at the interview on page 37 in the Student's Book. Answer the questions.

a Who is Jackson Miller? _____

b When did he first try skateboarding? _____

c What is the name of his new trick? _____

d When does he practice? _____

e What does he say about the Tampa Pro competition? _____

2 PLAN You are going to write an interview with a famous person who is good at something. Write his or her name in the graphic organizer. Use the notes to write your questions. Then, make notes for the answers.

INTERVIEW WITH _____

a What / good / at? _____
_____

b When / start / ...? _____
_____

c How long / take / learn? _____
_____

d How often / practice? _____
_____

e What / dream / future? _____
_____

3 WRITE Use your notes to write your interview. Think about how you will begin and end it. Add a photo if you have one.

4 EDIT Read your work and mark ✓.

Did you:

- introduce who you're interviewing? ☐
- ask interesting questions? ☐
- write appropriate answers? ☐
- use adjectives with prepositions? ☐

Ready to Read: Fiction

1 Key Words 4 **Match the words with the pictures.**

> beat echo crowd gather around tap disappointed

a

b

c

d

Hello.

Helloooooooo

e

f

___

2 **Choose the correct words to complete the sentences.**

> routine fascinating imitate make sure rhythm transport

a I think hip-hop music is _____ . I'm really interested in it.

b Jack clapped his hands to the _____ of the music.

c _____ you have everything you need. Have you checked?

d I don't like people who _____ others. They should have their own ideas.

e There was a bus to _____ us from the airport to the hotel.

f Some people like to have a daily _____ . They do the same things at the same time every day!

1. **Look at the picture. What do you think the story is about? Mark ✓. Then, read and check.**

   a a girl playing the piano with her grandmother ☐

   b a girl taking piano lessons ☐

   c a girl teaching a woman to play the piano ☐

Piano Keys

As soon as Roberta got off the bus, she realized she was going to be late. She ran down the street and knocked on the door of 11 Preston Drive. She was out of breath!

"Hello! I'm Roberta," she said to the woman who opened the door.

"Please come in!" said the woman, smiling. "I'm Mrs. Lang. Did you run all the way?"

"Hmmm, yes," said Roberta. "I got off the bus at the wrong stop!"

"Don't worry," Mrs. Lang said. "Let's get started."

Roberta was very excited. She and her grandmother visited one of her grandmother's friends on Preston Drive every month, and they often heard someone playing the piano at number 11. Roberta was fascinated. She thought it sounded beautiful.

"I'd love to play the piano," Roberta said to her grandmother. "Then, I could play in the next school concert. Could I take piano lessons?"

"Piano lessons are expensive," her grandmother said, "but I have an idea. Help me with my housework for three months, and I might pay for some lessons."

So every day for three months, Roberta cooked, cleaned, and helped her grandmother.

After three months, her grandmother said, "You've worked very hard. I can see you're serious about learning the piano. Here's the money for your first lesson. Mrs. Lang, the piano teacher who lives at number 11 Preston Drive, will give you your first lesson at 4 o'clock tomorrow."

And now Roberta was sitting at Mrs. Lang's piano.

"How well can you play, Roberta?" Mrs. Lang asked.

"Not at all," Roberta replied. "But my dream is to play in our school concert next summer!"

"That will take a lot of hard work. You'll have to practice every day."

In their first lesson, Mrs. Lang played a tune, and Roberta had to beat the rhythm with her hand. She did it well—she could feel the rhythm.

Then, Mrs. Lang played another tune, and Roberta copied it.

"You've done well," Mrs. Lang said at the end of the lesson. "I'll see you again next week. Remember to practice!"

And that is exactly what Roberta did. She practiced every day. By the end of the year, she could play beautifully!

At the school concert, she was the star of the show.

After the concert, Roberta hugged her grandmother. "Thank you for making my dream come true!"

SB pages 39–44

2 **Read the story again. Put the sentences in the correct order.**

a Roberta wanted to take piano lessons. ☐

b Roberta practiced until the end of the year. ☐

c Roberta and her grandmother heard someone playing the piano. [1]

d Roberta thanked her grandmother. [7]

e Roberta helped her grandmother with her housework for three months. ☐

f Roberta was the star of the school concert. ☐

g Roberta did well in her first piano lesson. ☐

> **Reading Strategy:** Literary Elements
>
> There are four elements in every story: the theme, the plot, the setting, and the characters.

3 **Complete the sentences about the theme, the plot, the setting, and the characters in the story.**

a The theme of the story is how important it is to practice if you want to do something well, like play the _____.

b Roberta is the main _____ of the story.

c Other characters help her. They are _____ and _____.

d The _____ of the story is how Roberta gets to take lessons with Mrs. Lang and becomes the star of the next school concert.

e The story is set mainly at _____.

4 **Why do you think Roberta's grandmother made her wait for three months before she gave her money for the piano lessons? Mark ✓.**

a She didn't have the money at first. ☐

b She wanted Roberta to learn about the value of money. ☐

c She wanted to make sure Roberta was serious about learning the piano. ☐

Might and could for Possibility

We can never be certain what will happen in the future, but, when we use *will*, we are more certain than when we use *might* and *could*.

I **might** pay for some piano lessons.

Then, I **could** play in the next school concert.

Mrs. Lang **will** give you your first lesson at 4 o'clock tomorrow.

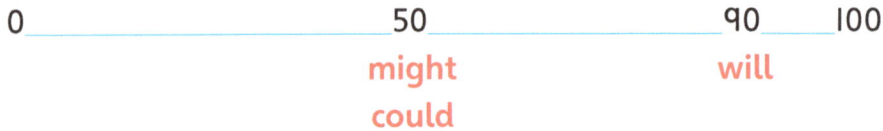

```
0_____50_____90____100
           might                      will
           could
```

1. Freddie has just joined a very good soccer team. Look at the sentences below. Label them *AC* (almost certain to happen) or *P* (only possible).

   a He'll be a good soccer player. ☐

   b He might play for his country. ☐

   c He could become famous. ☐

2. Write the words in the correct order. Then, label the sentences *AC* (almost certain to happen) or *P* (only possible).

   a later / You / could / study

   _____ ☐

   b finish / homework / dinner / might / my / before / I

   _____ ☐

   c be / at / My / will / home / 6 p.m. / sister

   _____ ☐

   d really / be / could / book / This / interesting

   _____ ☐

   e tomorrow / rain / might / It

   _____ ☐

   f next / will / brother / go / My / college / to / year

   _____ ☐

3 What are the children thinking? Write sentences.

athlete   astronaut   teacher   pilot

a Ariel

I _____

b Zahara

I _____

c Omar

I _____

d Juan

I _____

4 What will you do? What might or could you do? Write two sentences for each situation.

a   … when you have finished your homework?

_____

_____

b   … next weekend?

_____

_____

My Life

Write a verse for the poem "I Could Be Anything" that is true for you.

I could be a _____
And _____ .
Or I might be _____
And _____ .
But I am sure of one thing—
I will _____ .

Values: Keep Improving

1 **Think back to the *Piano Keys* story on page 32 and answer the questions.**

a What skill does Roberta want to keep improving? _____

b How does she do this? _____

c Can you give her advice? _____

2 **Which of these skills would you like to improve? Mark ✓. Can you think of two more?**

spelling ☐	handwriting ☐	English ☐	math ☐
SPELLING	Hand writing		$2 + 2 =$
swimming ☐	skateboarding ☐	singing ☐	drawing ☐
?		?	

3 **Write two skills you want to improve in the table. Then, write two ways you can improve each of those skills.**

Skills	I can do this by ...
1 I want to improve my _____ .	
2 I want to improve my _____ .	

36

How Did I Do?

Check Your Oracy: Ask Probing Questions

1	I asked probing questions.	**Many / Some / None**
2	I used the phrases on the cue cards.	**All of them / Most of them / Some of them**
3	My questions that got the longest answers were:	

The Big Challenge

How can we learn a new skill?

a **What skill are you going to learn?**

b **How well did you do? Color the stars to give yourself a score.***

I brainstormed new skills to learn.	☆☆☆☆☆
I chose a new skill and made a practice schedule.	☆☆☆☆☆
I presented my plan to the class.	☆☆☆☆☆
I reflected on the feedback.	☆☆☆☆☆

*(5 = Awesome! 4 = Pretty good, 3 = OK, 2 = Could be better, 1 = Needs more work!)

c **What could you do better next time?**

The Big Question and Me

Because of the things I have learned in this unit,

I will

1 Choose the correct words and write the jobs. There are two words you don't need.

> sculptor   astronaut   instructor   engineer   athlete   composer

a
b
c
d

a _____   b _____   c _____   d _____

2 Choose the correct words to complete the table.

> ambitions   creative   dedicated   disappointed   emotions

People have ...	People are ...

3 Choose the correct words to complete the text.

> college   curious   fascinating   patients   poison   routine   specialize

Hi! I'm Lianne, and I'm studying to be a veterinary nurse. I go to classes at my [1]_____ three days a week, and I study online at home. I also work part-time at a vet clinic. I have a busy life, so a [2]_____ is very important.
When I get to work, the first thing I do is check on the [3]_____. Many pet owners are very [4]_____ about animals, and they ask lots of questions. I want to [5]_____ in reptiles, like snakes and crocodiles.
I think they are [6]_____! I have to be careful because of the [7]_____. But if you're careful, it's OK.

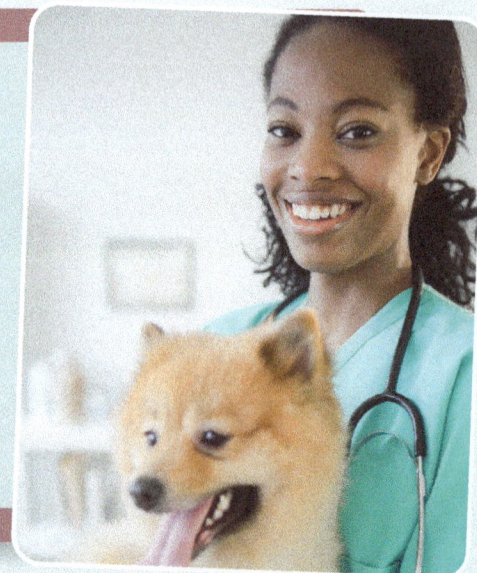

4 Look at the information about Jules and his family on the time line. Write sentences using the past simple and *ago*.

2010—a) Jules is born.

2011—b) Jules's family moves to Canada.

2012—c) Jules's mom gets a job at a design college as a teacher.

2013—d) Jules's dad gets his degree in mechanical engineering.

2017—e) Jules receives a ukulele as a birthday present.

2018—f) Jules wins a prize at school: "Best Ukulele Player."

a Jules was born ... years ago.

b _____

c _____

d _____

e _____

f _____

5 Jules is talking to his friend about the things he *might*, *could*, or *will* do in the future. Write his words in the correct order. Then, label the sentences AC (almost certain to happen) or P (only possible).

a Mexico / might / next / We / go / summer / to

_____ ☐

b could / we / go / But / the U.S.A. / to

_____ ☐

c Saturday / and / help / stay / home / mom / I'll / my / on

_____ ☐

6 Add the missing prepositions.

a My friends and I are interested _____ horseback riding.

b We never get bored _____ practicing.

c I think we're good _____ it because we win competitions!

SPEAKING MISSION

1 **Choose the correct words to complete the sentences.**

> advice   curious   drama   enjoy   options   recommended   suggestion   technology

a When you want to know or learn about something, you're _____ about it.

b My friend Zoe asked for my _____. I said she should talk to her mom about the problem.

c There are two _____. You can go to the movies or to the baseball game.

d Jessica was in a play at her high school last week. It was a fantastic _____.

d When you like doing something, you _____ it.

f The word "_____" refers to knowledge, equipment, and methods that are used in science and industry.

g I have a _____. Let's all go to the beach today.

h Jack _____ the movie. "It's excellent. You should see it," he said.

> What grade are you in?

> I'm in the fifth grade.

2 **Match the camp adviser's questions with the girl's answers.**

1 What grade are you in?
2 What are you interested in?
3 So, do you like swimming?
4 Are you good at biology?
5 Would you like to learn to scuba dive?
6 I recommend the adventure camp. Do you like that idea?

a I love it!
b I would love to learn that sport!
c I'm in the fifth grade.
d I'm interested in all water sports.
e Yes, thank you! I'm excited!
f Yes, I'm good at all science subjects.

What can you remember about Unit 2? Do the quiz.

1 Which of these questions about jobs was on page 28 in the Student's Book?

a Which job is your favorite?

b What makes each of these jobs difficult?

c Which job do you want to do when you leave school?

2 Which of these jobs did you not read about in Unit 2 in the Student's Book? Mark ✓.

astronaut ☐   artist ☐

composer ☐   firefighter ☐

professional soccer player ☐

travel writer ☐

zoo veterinarian ☐

3 Sophia, the reporter, interviewed Jackson Miller. What was the interview about?

a scuba diving

b skateboarding

c art

4 Gamelan music is from

_____ .

5 What is Ava very good at?

a science   b math   c spelling

6 This woman is an

_____ .

7 Write the words in the correct order.

a shark / saw / two years / I / an aquarium / visited / ago / when

_____

_____

8 How many literary elements are there in every story?

_____

9 What oracy skill did you learn to use in Unit 2? _____

10 Complete the sentence with the correct preposition.

My friend Marnie loves books. She never gets bored _____ reading!

Check your answers in the Student's Book. How did you do?

8–10 ☐ Wow!   6–7 ☐ Good job!   0–5 ☐ Try harder!

? 😄 How can we make our dreams come true? Write three things.

_____

_____

3 How can we deal with natural disasters?

1 ▶ 3.1 **Watch the video. Complete the graphic organizer.**

> droughts   earthquakes   floods   hurricanes   give national and international aid
> build better and stronger buildings   predict when a disaster is going to happen
> find other ways to help   tornadoes   volcanic eruptions

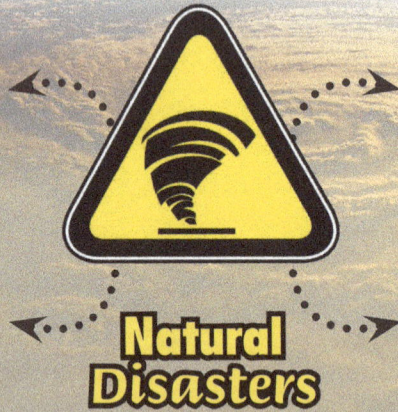

Earth-related events

_____

_____

Weather-related events

_____

_____

_____

_____

Natural Disasters

What can we do to prepare for natural disasters?

_____

_____

_____

What can we do after natural disasters?

_____

_____

_____

2 Key Words 1 **Complete the words. Then, match them with the pictures.**

1 v__lc__n__c __rupt____n ☐

2 ____rthq____k__ ☐

3 h__rr__c__n__ ☐

4 dr____ght ☐

5 ts__n__m__ ☐

6 t__rn__d__ ☐

 a ☐
 b ☐
 c ☐
 d ☐
 e ☐
 f ☐

Ready to Read: Nonfiction

1 `Key Words 2` **Label the diagrams.**

> crater   lava   magma   crust   mantle   core

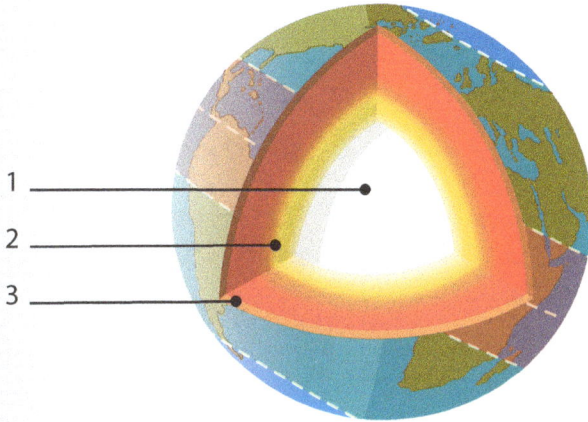

1
2
3

Inside the Earth

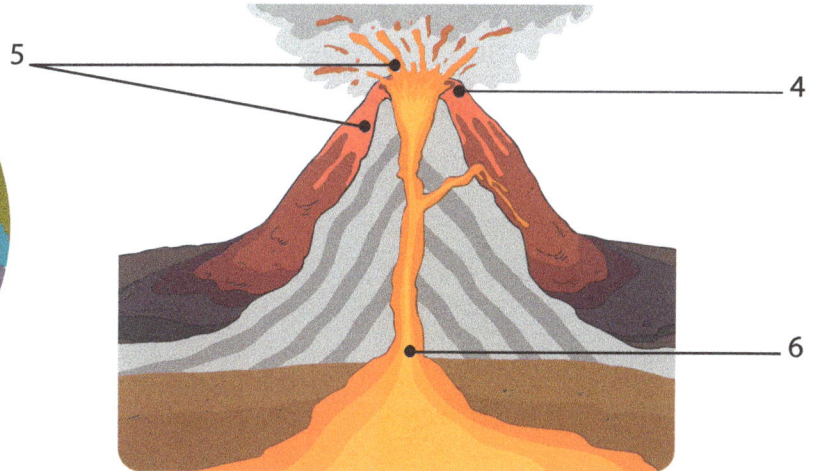

5
4
6

Inside a Volcano

2 **Choose the correct words to complete the sentences.**

> continental plates   friction   prevent   survivors

How can we ^{4} _____ these disasters?

As you know, there was an earthquake last year. There were many ^{1} _____ , but it was a disaster. Let's think about how earthquakes happen. There are two ^{2} _____ . When they move against each other, there is ^{3} _____ . When that is released, an earthquake happens. A disaster!

We must build stronger, safer buildings.

Reading Strategy: Using Graphic Sources

Remember to look at maps, charts, diagrams and their labels and captions when you read. They can help you understand and remember texts better.

1 **Match the questions with the graphic sources you need to answer them.**

1 Where are there the fewest historically active volcanoes?
2 What are the different types of volcanoes in the U.S.A.?
3 Where is the Ring of Fire?

a map
b bar graph
c pie chart

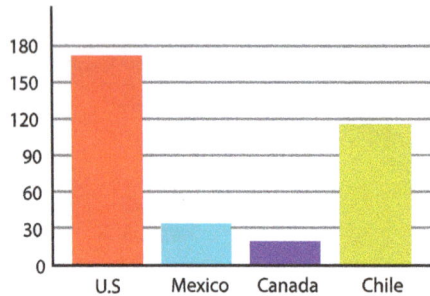

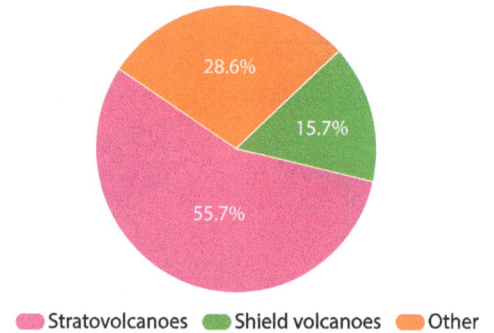

a Pacific Ring of Fire

b Active Volcanoes in the U.S.A., Mexico, Canada, and Chile

c U.S. Volcanoes by Type

Stratovolcanoes   Shield volcanoes   Other

2 **Read the article. Where are Mount Vesuvius, Mount St. Helens, and Mauna Loa?**

Vesuvius: _____ St. Helens: _____ Mauna Loa: _____

Volcanoes are very exciting but also very frightening. **What do you know about them?**

How Many Active Volcanoes Are There in the World?

There are about 500 active volcanoes in the world, and every year there are approximately 50 volcanic eruptions.

Where Are Most of the World's Volcanoes?

About 75% of the Earth's volcanoes are found around the Pacific Ocean. This circle of volcanoes is called the "Pacific Ring of Fire."

How Are Volcanoes Formed?

The Earth's crust has seven major continental plates and many more minor ones. These plates float on top of the magma, which flows under the crust. However, when there is a crack in the crust, the magma comes up through it in a volcanic eruption.

Shield Volcano or Stratovolcano?

There are different types of volcanoes. Two common ones are shield volcanoes and stratovolcanoes. Shield volcanoes are wide, and the lava comes out of them slowly when they erupt. Stratovolcanoes are shaped like cones and have more violent eruptions. They can send ash high up into the atmosphere.

Three Famous Volcanoes

Mount Vesuvius, in Italy, erupted in 79 CE. It covered the cities of Pompeii and Herculaneum with hot ash. There were no survivors. Vesuvius is a stratovolcano and is active today. It last erupted in 1944. It will erupt again. Smoke comes out of the crater every day.

In 1980, Mount St. Helens, in the state of Washington in the northwest of the U.S.A.,

3 Read the article again. Match the numbers with their meanings.

1 75   a the number of major continental plates on Earth
2 1980   b the approximate number of volcanic eruptions on Earth each year
3 50   c the percentage of the Earth's volcanoes in the "Pacific Ring of Fire"
4 500   d the number of active volcanoes on the planet
5 7   e the last time Mount St. Helens erupted

4 Circle the correct words.

a There are **many** / **a few** volcanoes in the "Pacific Ring of Fire."
b The text mentions **two** / **five** main types of volcanoes.
c Mount Vesuvius **will** / **will not** erupt again.
d The ash from the Mount St. Helens eruption in 1980 went nearly **30** / **50** km into the air.
e Mauna Loa means **Long** / **Big** Mountain.
f **Mount St. Helens** / **Vesuvius** erupted more recently than **Mount St. Helens** / **Vesuvius**.

5 Choose the best title for the article. Mark ✓.

Different Types of Volcanoes ☐   Let's Find Out About … Volcanoes ☐

Is There a Volcano Near You? ☐   Volcanoes and Earthquakes ☐

erupted violently. It is also a stratovolcano. The eruption sent lava down the mountain at over 460 kph. At the same time, ash went 26 km into the air. People felt the eruption in the state of Idaho and over 1,000 km away in the state of Montana.

The world's largest volcano is made up of a chain of volcanic islands. Mauna Loa, a shield volcano, is on the Big Island of Hawaii. It is one of the most active volcanoes on Earth. There have been 33 eruptions since 1843. It is 96 km long and 48 km wide. Its name means "Long Mountain" in Hawaiian.

Mauna Loa, a Shield Volcano

Mount Vesuvius, a Stratovolcano

The Present Simple Passive Voice

We use the passive voice when we don't know, or it isn't important, who did an action. We use *is/are* and the past participle. Always check the verb. Should it be *is* (singular) or *are* (plural)?

Passive	Active
Volcanoes are studied in elementary school.	The students study volcanoes in elementary school.
At Woodside Elementary School, the Mount St. Helens volcano is studied in 5th grade.	The students at Woodside Elementary School study the Mount St. Helens volcano in 5th grade.

1 **Circle the correct verb.**

a French, Italian, and German **is / are** spoken in Switzerland.

b Children **is / are** educated in schools.

c Soccer **is / are** played in many countries.

d Pasta **is / are** made with flour.

C'est un chat.

È un gatto.

Es ist eine Katze.

2 **Write the past participle of these verbs. Then, complete the school rules.**

clean _____   give _____

speak _____   wear _____

RULES

Uniforms are _____.

English is _____ in class.

Classrooms are _____ after school.

Homework is _____ on the weekends.

3 **Write sentences in the present simple passive.**

a The worksheets / print / in the office

  The worksheets are printed in the office.

b The car / wash / every weekend

  _____

c The horse / ride / every day

  _____

d The store / open / at 8:30 a.m. every day

  _____

e The house / clean / every week

  _____

4 **Write these present simple sentences in the passive.**

a The school children practice fire drills every semester.

Fire drills are practiced every semester.

b The teachers take the children outside the building.

_____

c The teachers take attendance.

_____

d Teachers check the building.

_____

5 **Complete the text with the correct present simple form of the verbs in parentheses.**

This week, **Appxpert Annie** writes about some great apps that
¹_____ (design) for emergencies.
No one wants to be in a disaster, but there are some great apps if you are ever in one.

EmergApp is an app where information about disasters in your area ²_____ (share). Posts ³_____ (make) by people when they see or experience something bad or dangerous.

FamApp ⁴_____ (use) to arrange a meeting place with your family.

CalmApp is a first aid app where important information about emergencies ⁵_____ (give).

Carrier 4:54 PM
CalmApp
Your First Aid Friend

What's your emergency?
Choose from the list for help.

Which do you think is the best app?

My Life

Design an emergency app for a flood, an earthquake, a tsunami, or a fire. Describe your app. Then, design an icon for it.

My app is called _____.

It is used to _____.

It has a special feature that is used for _____.

Spelling Patterns and Word Study

1 Look at the pictures and write the words. They all have the same *or* sound.

roar   shore   pour   floor

a

b

c

d

---

2 Look at the pictures. For each picture, circle the letters that make the *or* sound.

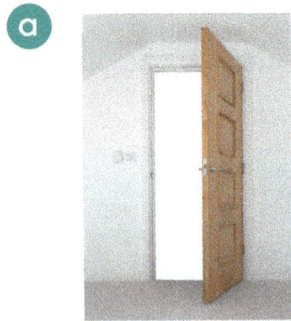

a

b

c

d

our   oar   ore   oor   our   oar   ore   oor   our   oar   ore   oor   our   oar   ore   oor

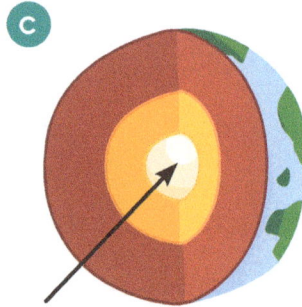

Oracy

1 Which one object did you talk about in Oracy Time? Why?

I talked about my _____ . I want to take it because

_____ .

2 Which one object did your partner talk about? Why?

My partner talked about his/her _____ . He/She wants to take it because

_____ .

3 Were you an active listener? What did you say? What did you do?

_____ .

Quotation Marks

Quotation marks are used to show that the words are spoken. You put marks like these " at the beginning and like these " at the end of someone's actual words. Put a capital letter at the beginning of the first word inside quotation marks. Remember the punctuation (exclamation marks, periods, etc.) goes inside the quotation marks.

Carol said, "That's a really great idea!"

1 **Read the short story. Color the words that are spoken.**

"Come on!" shouted Jake. "It's a really sunny day. Let's play soccer."

"Great idea," said Beatriz. "Mom? Where are my shoes?"

"Where you left them!" laughed Mom.

Then, Beatriz remembered her shoes were in her room. She ran upstairs and quickly put them on.

"Coming, Jake!" she shouted.

2 **Write these sentences with quotation marks and capital letters. Add punctuation where necessary.**

a Jake shouted that was a goal!

b Beatriz replied no, it wasn't.

c Markus said this is the best movie I've ever seen.

d I can't find my books anywhere cried Maria.

e I'm so tired said Mom.

Writing

1 **READ** Look at the news story on page 59 in the Student's Book. Circle the correct answer.

a There was a flood in **June / September** last year.

b The school lost **chairs and tables / the roof**.

c The floodwater took **two weeks / many months** to go away.

d It has taken a **long / short** time to clean up after the flood.

e The school has a new **library / classroom**.

f **Only local people / People from many places** gave money to help the school.

2 **PLAN** You are going to write a news story. Make notes in the graphic organizer.

HEADLINE (Make it interesting!)

_____

WHERE?

_____

WHAT?

_____

WHO?

_____

WHEN?

_____

WHO SAW IT HAPPEN, AND WHAT DID THEY SAY?

_____

_____

3 **WRITE** Use your notes to write your article.

4 **EDIT** Read your work and mark ✓.

Did you:

- write an interesting headline? ☐
- write a summary sentence to open? ☐
- answer all the questions? ☐
- use quotation marks? ☐

1 Key Words 4 **Match the word halves.**

a dea
b pan
c spin
d fun
e ca
f vio

lm
ic
nel
lent
dly
ning

2 **Choose the correct word to complete the sentences.**

debris   hail   howling   shattered   shelter   stripped

a During the storm, everyone went into the _____.

b Balls of ice that fall from the sky are called _____.

c The wind was _____ around the house during the storm.

d During a big weather event, windows are sometimes _____.

e There was a lot of _____ in the streets after the tornado.

f Trees lose their leaves in the fall—they are _____ by winds and storms.

3 **Circle the correct words.**

a A tornado is a **spinning** / **shattered** column of air.

b It is **funnel-** / **debris**-shaped.

c In an emergency, try to **panic** / **stay calm**.

d After a natural disaster, there is often a lot of **shelter** / **debris** to clean up.

e The people in the shelter heard the wind **howling** / **hailing**.

f During a tornado, trees are **stripped** / **spinning** of their leaves.

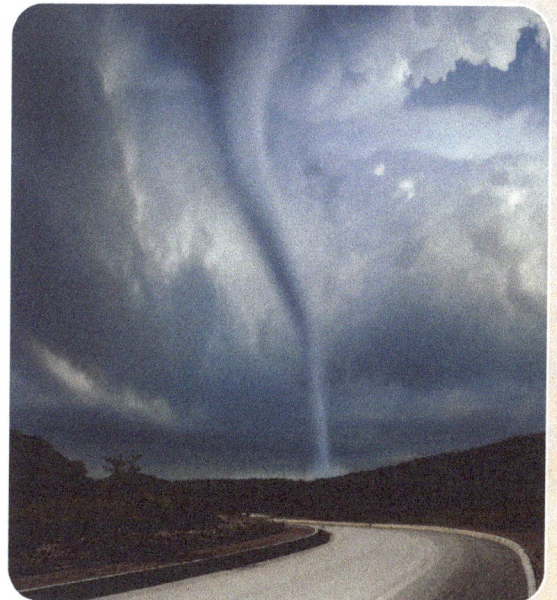

1 **Read the story. The children watched two TV programs. What were the programs about?**

Remi the Bear Goes on a Long Trip

Maggie ran into the family room. "Good morning, Jackson!" she shouted to her older brother. "What are we going to do today? Let's go outside and play."

"No, it's too cold to play outside," Jackson replied. "Let's watch TV."

"Oh, OK," said Maggie. She sat down on the sofa next to her brother. She was holding her favorite toy, a very old teddy bear called Remi. The children watched a TV program about animals. They both loved animals. Then, the program changed, and there was a news report.

"OK," said Jackson, getting up from the sofa. "This is really boring."

But Maggie was interested. "Wait," she said. "Look at those children. What happened?"

Jackson sat down again. They watched the news together. It was about a natural disaster.

"A deadly tornado hit this beautiful Pacific island yesterday and destroyed everything in its path. Many people didn't reach the shelters in time. There is debris everywhere," said the reporter.

Jackson said, "Those children look scared."

"Yes," Maggie said. "We have to do something. But what can we do?"

The reporter continued, "Clothes, toys, and books are needed here. Please help. The supermarket Food4U will deliver everything to the island. Go online to find your nearest Food4U. Anything you can give will be welcome."

The children ran up to their bedrooms. They collected lots of clothes, toys, and books for the children on the island. Mom heard them.

"What's happening up there?" she asked.

Jackson explained, and Maggie said, "We have too many clothes and toys. We want to give some to those children, Mom. Can you take us to the Food4U in town, please?"

The supermarket was very busy. A tall, friendly man came up to them.

"Did you bring things for the survivors of the disaster?" he asked.

"Yes, we did," said Jackson.

"That's great," the man said. "Thank you very much. Please put them over there."

"Do you have enough things for the children now?" Maggie asked.

"Well, there are enough things for older children, but we don't have enough toys for younger children," the man replied.

Maggie looked at Remi. "Goodbye, Remi," she said.

She gave the man her teddy bear and said, "This is Remi. He wants to help the children."

Jackson looked at his sister. "You're very generous, Maggie," he said quietly.

She smiled and said, "I really want to help those children."

Explore the Text

2 Read the story again. Put the events in order.

a   The children went up to their bedrooms.   ◯

b   Maggie gave the man at the supermarket her favorite toy, Remi the Bear.   ◯

c   The reporter on the news talked about a natural disaster.   ◯

d   The children watched a program about animals.   ◯

e   It was a very cold day.   ◯

f   The children's mom drove them to the supermarket.   ◯

Reading Strategy: Visualizing

When you visualize, you see a picture in your head. This helps you to understand, remember, and enjoy the story.

3 Visualize the Food4U supermarket and answer the questions. Then, add more information to the story.

1   What do you think Maggie and Jackson can:

   a   hear? _____

   b   smell? _____

   c   see? _____

2   How do you think they feel?

_____

_____

_____

_____

MAGGIE AND JACKSON AT THE SUPERMARKET
There are lots of people at the Food4U supermarket. They are giving clothes, books, toys, and food.

_____

_____

_____

_____

4 Why do you think Maggie gave her teddy bear to the man at the supermarket?

_____

Grammar in Context

Too and enough

We use *too* and *enough* to suggest comparative amounts.

It's too cold to play outside.

It was warm enough in the classroom.

Before nouns, we use *enough*, *too much*, or *too many*.

We have too many clothes and toys.

There are enough things for older kids, but there aren't enough toys for younger kids.

1 **Look at the pictures. Circle the correct words.**

a

Is that OK?

No, that's **enough / too much** ketchup.

b

There are **too many / too much** cars on the roads!

c

Would you like a pencil?

No, thanks. I have **enough / too much** pencils.

d

Try this shoe! That one is **too / enough** small.

2 **Write the words in the correct order.**

a too / It's / hot / outside _____

b money / have / We / enough / don't _____

c I / food / enough / have _____

d too / There / many / are / people _____

e cake / I / sugar / much / in / this / too / put _____

f chairs / The / enough / room / has _____

3 **Match the pairs of sentences.**

1 It's too dark in here.
2 It's too cold outside.
3 This watch is very expensive.
4 She is very young.
5 My bicycle can't be fixed.

a It costs too much money.
b There isn't enough light to see.
c She isn't old enough to go on the rollercoaster.
d There are too many things broken on it.
e Our clothes aren't warm enough.

4 Choose the correct words to complete the sentences. Some are used more than once.

> too   enough   too much   too many

a He has _____ toys.

b He got _____ presents. When will he play with them all?

c There's _____ food. He can't eat it all!

d There are _____ drinks. He can't drink them all!

e The bag is _____ heavy. I can't lift it.

f Can we do this later? I don't have _____ time to finish it now.

5 Answer the questions. Use the words in parentheses.

a Why can't the horse jump over the gate? (too)

The gate _____.

b Why can't the boy lift 200 kg? (enough)

He _____.

c Why can't the cat catch the mouse? (enough)

It _____.

d Why can't the boy wake up? (too)

He _____.

My Life

Complete the sentences so that they are true for you.

I have too many _____.

I have too much _____.

I have enough _____.

I don't have enough _____.

55

1 How do you help at home? Mark ✓.

Do you:

wash the dishes? ☐   cook? ☐   sweep the floor? ☐   water plants in the yard? ☐

2 How are the people helping? Write five sentences.

> collect / shopping carts   sell / hot dogs to help earthquake survivors
> call / ambulance   pick up / baby's toy   buy / hot dog to help earthquake survivors

"Ambulance, please, quickly!"

a A man is calling for an ambulance.

b Another man _____ .

c A girl _____ .

d Two girls _____ .

e Jen _____ .

3 When was the last time you helped someone? What did you do? Write a sentence.

_____

How Did I Do?

3

Check Your Oracy: Active Listening

1	I looked at my partner while we were talking.	All the time / Most of the time / Sometimes
2	I showed interest by asking questions.	Yes, a lot. / Yes, sometimes.
3	I used the phrases on the cue cards.	All of them / Most of them / Some of them

The Big Challenge — STEAM: Technology & Engineering

How can we invent a device to help people after a natural disaster?

a What device did you invent?

_____

b How well did you do? Color the stars to give yourself a score.*

I researched different devices.	☆ ☆ ☆ ☆ ☆
I brainstormed new ideas	☆ ☆ ☆ ☆ ☆
I designed my device.	☆ ☆ ☆ ☆ ☆
I presented my disaster aid device to the class.	☆ ☆ ☆ ☆ ☆

*(5 = Awesome! 4 = Pretty good, 3 = OK, 2 = Could be better, 1 = Needs more work!)

c Which other device did you like the best?

_____

d What could you do better next time?

_____

The Big Question and Me

Because of the things I have learned in this unit,

I will _____

_____

57

SB pages 68–69

1 **Match the words with the pictures.**

1 drought
2 earthquake
3 hurricane
4 tornado
5 tsunami
6 volcanic eruption

2 **Unscramble these words. Then, label the diagrams.**

a aamgm
_____

c alva
_____

e sutcr
_____

b acrtre
_____

d erco
_____

f atemln
_____

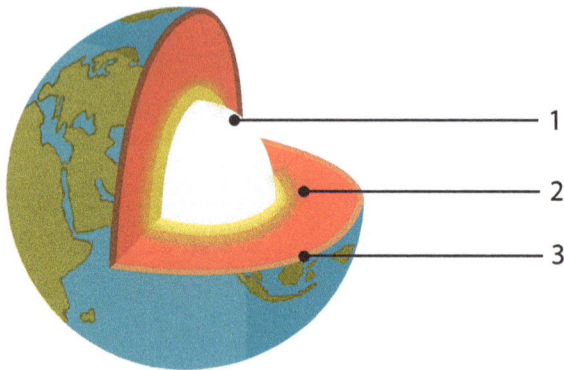

3 **Choose the correct words to complete the sentences.**

architect   demolish   drill   resistant

a An _____ is a person who designs buildings.

b In some places, buildings have to be earthquake-_____.

c You have to _____ damaged buildings when you can't rebuild them.

d Many schools have a fire _____ several times a semester.

4 Complete the paragraphs with the present simple passive of the verbs in parentheses.

In some parts of the world, when a tornado or a hurricane is coming, a bell
1_____ (ring). In schools, children 2_____ (teach) emergency drills. Storm shelters
3_____ (build) in the backyards of houses to protect people.

When there is a natural disaster, many emergency services 4_____ (involve).
Here, a doctor 5_____ (need) to treat people who are injured. Survivors
6_____ (find) by the fire department.

5 Complete the sentences with *too* or *enough*.

a I don't understand. You're speaking _____ quickly.

b We don't need to buy any more food. There's _____ food here.

c Let's stay inside. It's _____ hot outside.

d I don't have _____ time now. Can we talk about this later?

e There are _____ many people here. Let's go home.

f I can buy this. I have _____ money.

6 Put quotation marks in the correct places in these sentences.

We're ready to talk about our emergency device, said the children.

What do you think? asked Janice.

What a great presentation! said the teacher. Well done!

1 What were the five most important items your group chose for your emergency kit? Which was the most important of all? Say why.

1 _____

2 _____

3 _____

4 _____

5 _____

I think _____ is the most important of all because

_____ .

2 What is the second speaker (B) doing in these dialogues? Mark ✓.

A I think we should take a flashlight. → **B** Why do you think that?

1 a She's asking a probing question. ☐
   b She's giving her opinion. ☐

A I think we should take a flashlight. → **B** That's a good idea.

2 a She's asking a probing question. ☐
   b She's listening actively. ☐

3 Write the words in the correct order.

a because … / this / think / I

_____ .

b repeat / Can / that / you

_____ ?

c about … / think / you / do / What

_____ ?

d questions / any / have / you / Do

_____ ?

4 Write your favorite …

ground rule. _____

probing question. _____

phrase to show you are actively listening. _____

What can you remember about Unit 3? Do the quiz.

1 What three graphic sources did you use when you read the text about volcanoes?

_____

_____

2 What is this?

_____

_____

3 What is the missing word?

This picture shows the core, the mantle, and the _____

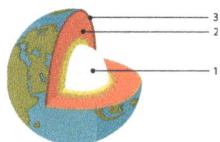

4 What are the missing words?

When there is an earthquake, the _____

_____ move.

5 What natural disaster was Fluffy the hamster involved in?

_____

6 Write the missing word.

The information _____ used to help us understand natural disasters.

7 Rewrite this sentence using the present simple passive.

People design many earthquake-resistant buildings these days.

_____

_____

8 Circle the correct word.

I can't buy that phone.
It's **too / enough** expensive.

9 What oracy skill did you learn in Unit 3?

_____

_____

10 Put the quotation marks in the correct place.

Hey! I'm here! Help me! shouted Olivia. I can't see the door. It's very dark.

Check your answers in the Student's Book. How did you do?

8–10 ☐ Wow!   6–7 ☐ Good job!   0–5 ☐ Try harder!

? 😃 How can we deal with natural disasters? Write three things.

_____

_____

_____

4 What makes going to a show so exciting?

1 ▶ **4.1** **Watch the video. Complete the graphic organizer with the characteristics of four of the shows.**

wear 3D glasses and seat belts   live actors and actresses   physical sensations
listen to your favorite artists   gigantic video screens   acrobats
lots of makeup   on a stage in a theater

a

_____
_____

Play _____

b

Enhanced Movie _____

Shows and Their Characteristics

c

Outdoor Concert _____

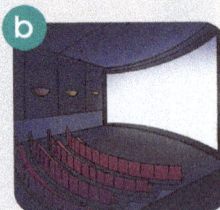

d

Circus _____

_____
_____

2 **Key Words 1** **Choose the correct words to complete the sentences.**

props   actors   costume   show   fireworks   makeup   live performances   special effects

| a This woman is putting on a lot of _____. | b These _____ are amazing! | c She's wearing a great _____, and her _____ are good, too. | d Look at the _____! I love _____! | e Wow! Look at the _____! The _____ is starting! |

SB pages 72–73

1 Key Words 2 **Write the words in the correct places.**

puppet theater   audience   musical   opera   puppeteers   stage

a _____

b _____

c _____

d _____

e _____

f _____

2 **Circle the correct words to complete the paragraph.**

I saw a new play at the theater last week. It was really good, but it was very sad. It was a
[1]**tragedy / comedy.** At times, no one spoke. That's [2]**mime / stage.** When the people were
speaking, the [3]**stage / dialogue** was interesting! Next week we're going to see a different
show. It's a [4]**comedy / musical,** so there will be lots of singing! My friend has seen it. It
starts with an empty [5]**stage / opera,** and then lots of people come on and do [6]**acrobatics /
audience.** My friend said the [7]**stage / audience** clapped for a long time when she saw it!

1 **What types of dancing can you see in the photos? Read the article and write the names.**

a _____

b _____

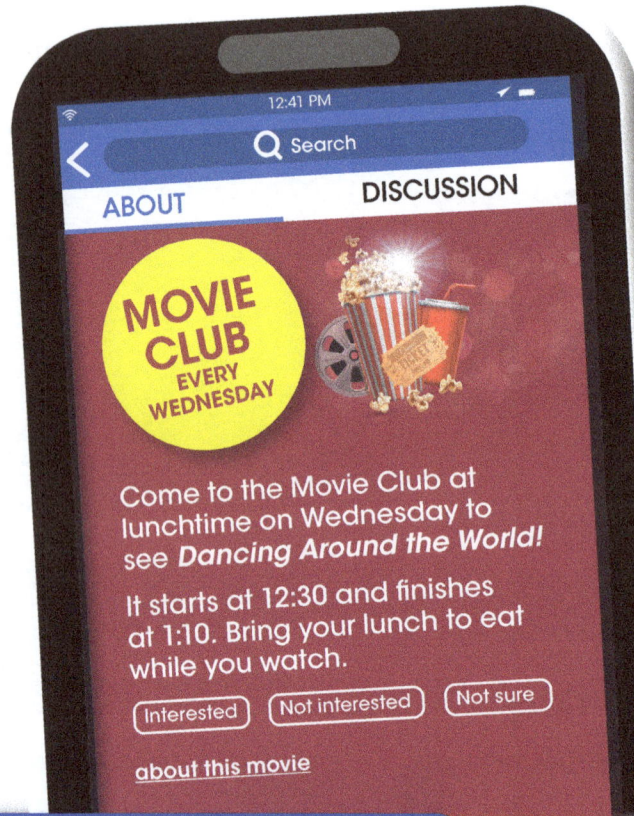

12:41 PM

Q Search

ABOUT   DISCUSSION

MOVIE CLUB
EVERY WEDNESDAY

Come to the Movie Club at lunchtime on Wednesday to see *Dancing Around the World!*

It starts at 12:30 and finishes at 1:10. Bring your lunch to eat while you watch.

(Interested)   (Not interested)   (Not sure)

about this movie

c _____

d _____

Dancing Around The World: A Must-see Movie

Did you know that there are cave paintings in India that are over 9,000 years old, and they show people dancing? Over the centuries, there have been many different types of dance. *Dancing Around the World* will show you four exciting kinds that may be new to you: Capoeira, tap, Bollywood, and Cossack dancing.

Capoeira is from Brazil. It began in the 16th century, and it mixes acrobatics, dance, martial arts, and music. The dancers have to be in very good shape. They are more like athletes than dancers. They "fight" each other. The audience stands in a circle around the dancers, and people clap out the rhythm of the dance.

Have you seen the film *Happy Feet* with its **tap dancing** penguins? Tap dancing became popular in the 19th century, but it probably began long before that. In the middle of the 20th century there was a lot of tap dancing in movies, but it isn't so popular now. Like Capoeira dancers, tap dancers often used to dance in pairs to "fight" each other. Tap dancers wear special shoes with metal "taps" on them to make a noise on the floor. Tap dancers can move their feet really fast!

Bollywood dancing comes from India. You can see it in many Bollywood movies. It mixes traditional and modern Indian dances and sometimes dances from other countries, too, like R&B, jazz, and funk.

SB pages 74–77

2 Read the text again and write the answers.

a Which dancers wear special shoes? _____

b What do these shoes do? _____

c Which dance gets quicker and quicker? _____

d Which dance is from India? _____

e Who first did Cossack dancing? _____

f In which two dances do the dancers "fight" each other? _____

> **Reading Strategy:** Summarizing (Nonfiction)
>
> A summary is a short description. When you summarize a nonfiction text, you should: underline the main ideas and important words in the text, retell the main ideas in your own words, and only include important details.

3 You read about *Dancing Around the World* on your phone. Your teacher asked you to write a summary of the part about Bollywood dancing. Circle the correct words.

Bollywood dancing is from [1]**India / Ukraine.** You can see it in many [2]**operas / movies.** It mixes traditional and modern Indian dancing with dances from other countries, such as [3]**jazz / ballet.** The dancers wear [4]**gray / beautiful** costumes. It's [5]**boring / fun** to watch.

4 Complete the sentence so that it is true for you.

I would like to see _____ dancing because

_____ .

Bollywood dancing is a lot of fun to watch, and the costumes are always beautiful and colorful.

Cossack dancing began in Ukraine in the 16th century. When soldiers won a battle, they celebrated by dancing and jumping high in the air. Some of them played musical instruments, and others danced. The music has a very strong beat, which gets faster and faster. It's very exciting to watch. Like Capoeira performers and tap dancers, the people who do Cossack dancing have to be in very good shape. Perhaps you've seen Cossack dancing in one of the *Indiana Jones* movies.

Grammar in Context

Present Simple for Future Events

We use the present simple to talk about future events that have a timetable. We are very certain that they will happen.

Dancing Around The World **starts** at 12:30 on Wednesday.

1 Write the words in the correct order.

a Chicago / The / at / train / 5:28 p.m. / leaves / to

_____

b comes / bus / next / The / minutes / ten / in

_____

c day / tomorrow / What / is / it?

_____

d in / starts / party / Harry's / minutes / five

_____

e new class / the / end of January / at / starts / The

_____

2 Complete the sentences about the future. Write the correct form of the verbs in parentheses.

a The music festival _____ (end) next Sunday.

b The play _____ (start) in two minutes.

c My sister's birthday _____ (be) on Friday.

d The train _____ (arrive) in London at 10:35 tomorrow morning.

e What day _____ (open / the new show) next week?

f What time _____ (open / the library) tomorrow?

3 Which sentences are about the future? Mark ✓.

a I'm reading an interesting book at the moment. ☐

b The bus leaves at 10 a.m. tomorrow. ☐

c My math class finishes at 3:30 this afternoon. ☐

d I studied all day. ☐

e Our field trip was to the city museum. ☐

f The exam starts at 9 a.m. on Friday. ☐

66

SB page 78

4 Read the dialogue and complete the poster.

Mom What day is your play on?

Ed On Saturday.

Mom What time does it start?

Ed At 6 p.m.

Mom And what time does it end?

Ed At about 7:30 p.m.

Mom I'm really looking forward to it!

Grade 5 presents:

Lakeview School

This Is Our Time

On ¹_____, March 3

At ²_____ in the school theater

Running Time: ³_____ minutes

5 Read the email. Write questions and answers in the dialogue.

Dear Parents,

Here is the information about the field trip to see the musical *Aladdin* next Tuesday.

- The bus leaves school at 10 a.m.
- We arrive at the park for lunch at 12 o'clock.
- The show starts at 2 p.m.
- The bus leaves the theater at 4:30 p.m.
- We arrive back at school at 6:30 p.m.

If you have any questions, please email me.

Sincerely,

Sheila Jones

Principal

a What time / bus / school?

_____

At _____

b When / they / have lunch?

_____

At _____

c What time / musical / start?

_____

At _____

d When / bus / leave the theater?

_____

At _____

e What time / they / arrive back at school?

_____

At _____

My Life

Find out about a show or movie in your town.

What time does it start?

_____

When does it finish?

_____

What day is it on?

_____

4A

Spelling Patterns and Word Study

1 **Look at the pictures and write the words. They all have the same sound.**

shadow   piano   shoulder   road

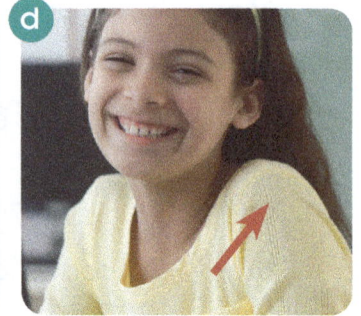

a _____

b _____

c _____

d _____

2 **Look at the pictures. Circle the correct spelling pattern for the word.**

a   ow   oe   ou   o   oa   c   ow   oe   ou   o   oa

b   ow   oe   ou   o   oa   d   ow   oe   ou   o   oa

Oracy

1 **Which Oracy Time! topic did your group discuss? Mark ✓ and write the name.**

movie ☐ _____   musical group ☐ _____

singer ☐ _____   athlete ☐ _____

actor ☐ _____   actress ☐ _____

2 **What reasons did you give when you expressed your point of view?**

_____

_____ .

3 **What did you say when you agreed or disagreed with the people in your group? Mark ✓ the phrases you used and write complete sentences.**

☐ In my opinion, _____ .

☐ I agree because _____ .

☐ I disagree because _____ .

Conjunctions

We use connecting words (or conjunctions) to make two sentences into one sentence.

I like musicals. I love operas. = I like musicals, and I love operas.

I like musicals. I don't like plays. = I like musicals, but I don't like plays.

I like musicals. I'm going to see a musical. = I like musicals, so I'm going to see a musical.

1 **Match the conjunctions with their meanings.**

1	so	a	adds information
2	and	b	contrasts information
3	but	c	shows the consequence of something

2 **Read the dialogue and circle the correct conjunction.**

David What are you doing this weekend?

Juliana I don't have any fun plans. I have a lot of homework, ¹ **and / so** I have a test next week, ² **but / so** I have to study.

David Look at this! It's a new play. I'm going on Saturday night, ³ **and / but** my parents have invited you to come along with us.

Juliana That's great! I'd love to! I can come if I work hard during the day on Saturday.

David OK. It will be my parents, you, and me, ⁴ **so / and** my cousin, Billie, is coming, too.

Juliana Sounds good. Thanks, David. Now it's time for my bus, ⁵ **so / but** I have to go. Bye!

David See you on Saturday!

3 **Write the best conjunction.**

a I enjoy watching movies, _____ I prefer playing video games.

b I enjoy opera, _____ I enjoy ballet.

c I was hungry, _____ I ate a big sandwich!

d My sister is great at soccer and basketball, _____ she isn't good at tennis.

e We wanted to buy some tickets, _____ there weren't any left!

f We were very late, _____ we had to run to catch the train.

1 READ Look at the movie review on page 81 in the Student's Book. Answer the questions.

a What is the title of the movie? _____

b Who are the main characters? _____

c What does the author like about the movie? _____

_____

d What does the author dislike about it? _____

2 PLAN You are going to write a movie review. Make notes in the graphic organizer.

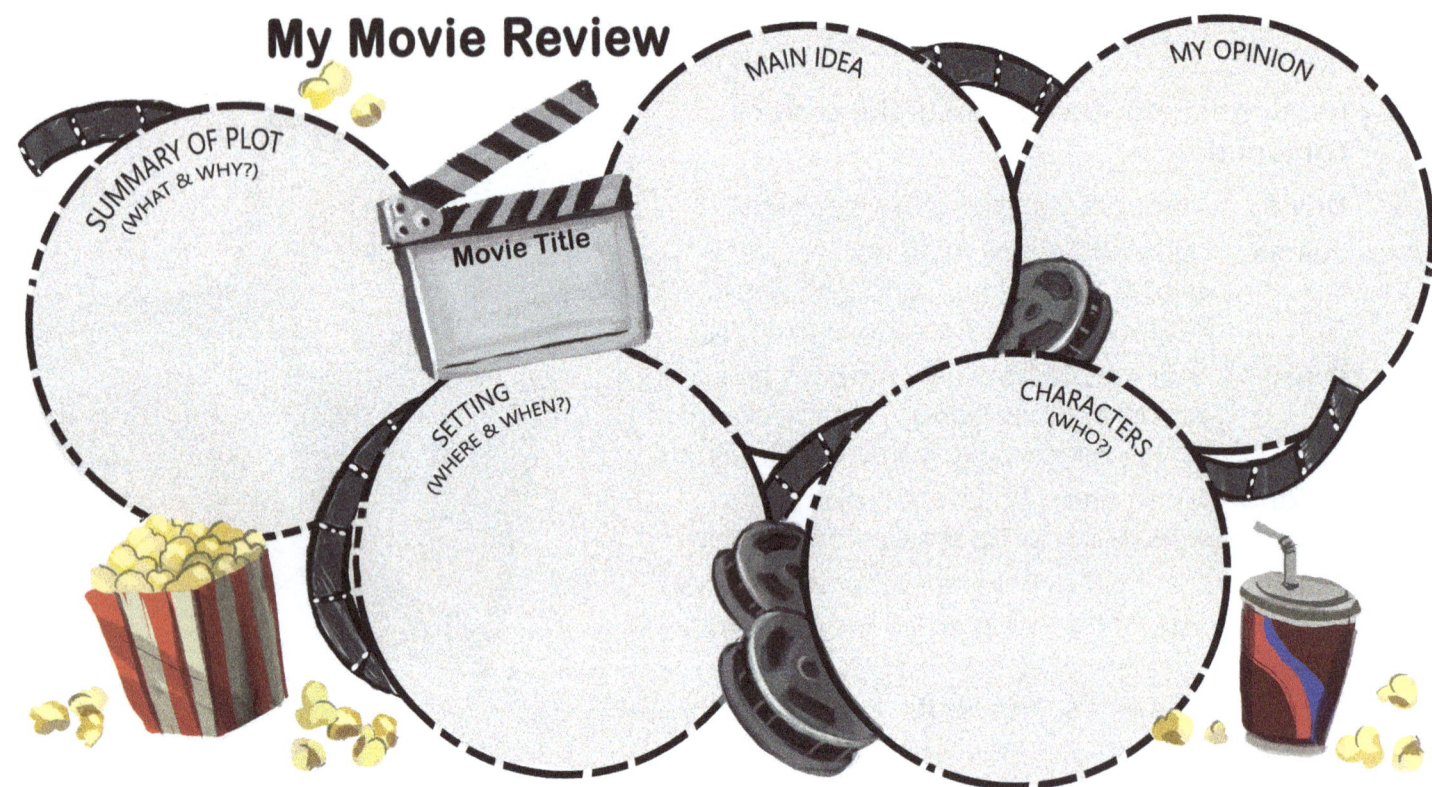

My Movie Review

SUMMARY OF PLOT
(WHAT & WHY?)

MAIN IDEA

MY OPINION

Movie Title

SETTING
(WHERE & WHEN?)

CHARACTERS
(WHO?)

3 WRITE Use your notes to write your review.

4 EDIT Read your work and mark ✓.

Did you:

• describe the movie and characters? ☐
• say what's good and bad about it? ☐

• give your opinion? ☐
• use conjunctions? ☐

1 ⟨Key Words 4⟩ **Choose the correct words to complete the sentences.**

attic   bandits   crime   driveway   guilty   scratch

a Look at this _____ on the table! Who did it?

b The _____ up to Mr. Bartlett's house is very long.

c Some _____ wear masks so that you can't see their faces.

d The part of the house under the roof is called the _____ .

e "I know you took the chocolates! You look very _____!"

f Which police officer solved the _____ ?

2 **Complete the puzzle. What is I down?**

Across

2 Three people born on the same day who have the same mother.

3 This proves that a person was not in the place where a crime happened, so he or she cannot be guilty of that crime.

4 This is a piece of information that helps you solve a problem or answer a question.

5 A mark on a smooth, flat surface that makes it look bad.

6 The mark you make with your foot.

7 When something or someone is messy or doesn't make good plans.

8 You can wear these on your feet.

Down

I This is a _____ .

1 **Read the story. Put the pictures in the correct order.**

Learning Your Lines

Madison, Michael, and Matt, the Mills triplets, were talking about the last rehearsal of *This Is Our Time.*

"The play starts tomorrow. Do you think Jake has learned his lines yet?" Madison asked her brothers on the way to the theater.

"He said he knew them yesterday …," Michael said.

"… but he didn't," Matt added. Matt always finished Michael's sentences. "Ms. Black won't be happy if he hasn't learned them."

When they got to the theater, all the actors and actresses were on stage warming up. The beginning of the rehearsal was going well. Everyone seemed to know their lines. But suddenly, there was silence. Everyone looked at Jake, and Jake looked embarrassed.

"Jake, you have to learn your lines!" Ms. Black wasn't happy. "Everyone needs to know their lines for tomorrow!"

Jake stared at the floor. "I know," he said quietly. "I've tried to learn them, but I just can't."

As everyone was leaving, the triplets ran up to Jake.

"Jake," Madison said, "we can help you. We'll come over to your house, OK?"

"Uh, sure," said Jake.

"Don't worry …" Michael said.

"… we have a trick. It works every time," Matt continued.

Soon after, Jake met the triplets in his driveway, and they all headed up to his room in the attic.

"OK, what's the trick?"

"First, we need some paper—three sheets," Madison said.

Jake looked surprised, but he took three pieces of paper out of his desk.

"OK, here's the paper. What do I do with it?"

"You make a footprint with your sneakers on each sheet …" directed Michael.

"… and write your lines on the footprints," said Matt.

"Then, read each set of lines and step on them when you finish," said Madison.

Jake practiced all night long: left foot, right foot, left foot …. And, what do you know? It worked! The next day, he didn't forget a single word! Ms. Black even said he was one of the best in the show. Thrilled, he ran up to the triplets. "Thank you so much! But I don't get it. How does the trick work?"

"It's simple," said Michael. "You connect each step you make …"

"… with each set of lines," Matt interrupted.

Jake was glowing with pride when saw his parents after the show. They congratulated him on his performance. "Well done, Jake, you were fantastic!" his mom said.

2 **Read the story again. Put the events in order.**

a   Jake remembered all his lines. ☐

b   The triplets went to Jake's house. ☐

c   Ms. Black was angry with Jake. ☐

d   The beginning of the rehearsal went well. ☐

e   Jake wrote his lines on the footprints. ☐

f   The triplets talked about Jake's problem before the rehearsal. ☐

g   Jake made three footprints on the paper with his sneakers. ☐

h   Jake was silent on the stage. ☐

Reading Strategy: Summarizing (Fiction)

A summary of a fiction text is a short description of the story. It tells us about the main characters, the problem, and how the problem is solved.

3 **Complete the table for the story.**

Summary Chart: Learning Your Lines	
Somebody Who is the main character?	
But What was the problem?	
So How was the problem solved?	
Then How did the story end?	

4 **How do you remember new words? Mark ✓. If you can, add one of your own ideas.**

Do you ...

draw a picture? ☐

say the words lots of times? ☐

write the words in a book? ☐

I sometimes _____ .

Subject and Object Questions

We use subject questions to find out who or what does something.

Matt always finished Michael's sentences.

Who always finished Michael's sentences? } SUBJECT
Matt did.

We use object questions to find out about what someone or something does.

What did Matt finish? } OBJECT
Michael's sentences.

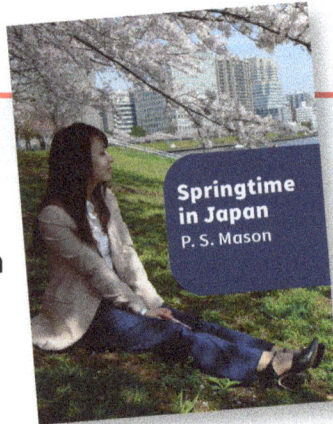

BOOK REVIEW

The new book by the world-famous author P. S. Mason is set in Japan. The main character, Kimiko, lives in Tokyo. She is an elementary school teacher. She teaches eight-year-old children.

1 **Look at the book cover and read the beginning of the book review. Match the questions with the answers. Which are subject questions (S)? Which are object questions (O)? Write S or O.**

1 Who wrote this book? ☐   a Eight-year-old children

2 What did P. S. Mason write? ☐   b Kimiko

3 Who lives in Tokyo? ☐   c P. S. Mason

4 Who does Kimiko teach? ☐   d A book about Japan

2 **Read the sentences and write a subject and an object question for each one. Use *Who* or *What*. Then, answer the questions.**

a The triplets helped Jake.

Who helped Jake?

The triplets did.

_____ did the triplets help?

_____ .

b Jake wrote his lines in the footprints.

_____ wrote his lines in the footprints?

_____ .

_____ did Jake write in the footprints?

_____ .

c Jake thanked Madison, Michael, and Matt.

_____ thanked Madison, Michael, and Matt?

_____ .

_____ did Jake thank?

_____ .

3 Read and complete the puzzle. Then, write two questions for the sentences.

George called Fred, but Bill called George. Jack called Bill, and Fred called Jack.

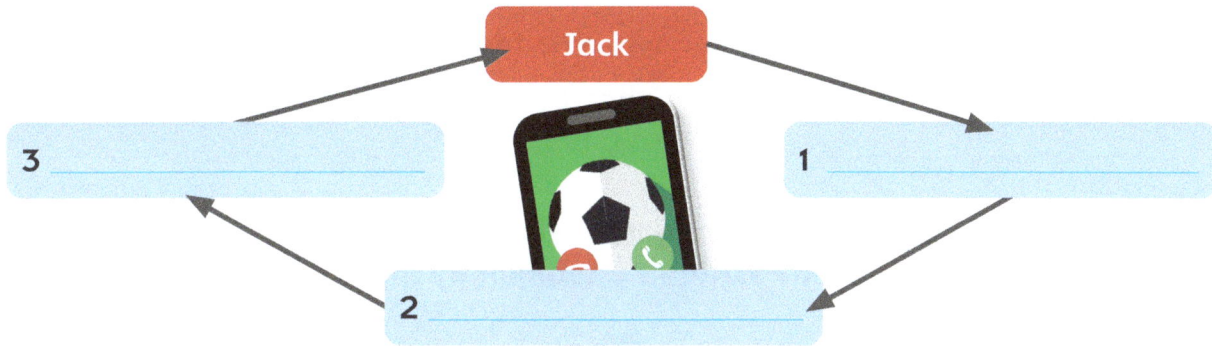

Jack

3 _____

1 _____

2 _____

a George called Fred.

Who called Fred?

Who did George call?

b Bill called George.

_____

_____

c Jack called Bill.

_____

_____

d Fred called Jack.

_____

_____

4 Write questions about the underlined words.

a Mike ate the <u>chocolates</u>.

_____

b Susie talked to <u>Rafaello</u>.

_____

c <u>Margot</u> made her own lunch.

_____

d <u>The earthquake</u> damaged the house.

_____

My Life

Write about yesterday.

What happened to you? _____

Who did you talk to? _____

Who talked to you? _____

What did you see? _____

1 **Think back to the *Learning Your Lines* story on page 72. Circle the correct answer to the questions.**

1   What did Jake have to do?   2   Which was more successful?

   a   sing a song   a   when he tried to learn them by himself

   b   learn his lines for a play   b   when the triplets helped him and they worked as a team

2 **Look at the pictures. Which activities are better when you work as a team? Which are better when you work by yourself? Write *As a team* or *By myself* and say why.**

a    b    c 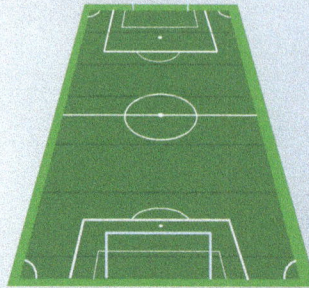   d

because _____   because _____   because _____   because _____

3 **Why do you think working as a team is good? Mark ✓ the points you agree with and add your own ideas.**

You can share ideas. ☐

It can be more fun. ☐

Different people have different talents. ☐

My ideas: _____

_____

_____

4 **Do you usually prefer to work by yourself or as a team? Why?**

_____

_____

_____

Check Your Oracy: Expressing Points of View

1	I confidently expressed my point of view and used reasons.	All the time / Most of the time / Sometimes
2	I listened actively when others expressed their points of view.	All the time / Most of the time / Sometimes
3	I gave reasons when I agreed or disagreed with my group members.	All the time / Most of the time / Sometimes

The Big Challenge   STEAM: Technology & Art

How can we perform a song in English?

a   **Which song did you perform?**

_____

b   **How well did you do? Color the stars to give yourself a score.***

I planned my performance	☆☆☆☆☆
I practiced my performance.	☆☆☆☆☆
I performed my song in front of the class.	☆☆☆☆☆
I gave feedback to other singers with my reasons.	☆☆☆☆☆

*(5 = Awesome! 4 = Pretty good, 3 = OK, 2 = Could be better, 1 = Needs more work!)

c   **Which other performance did you like the best?**

_____

d   **What could you do better next time?**

_____

The Big Question and Me

Because of the things I have learned in this unit,

I will _____

_____

1 Match the words with the pictures.

> driveway   puppeteer   costumes   props   fireworks   scratch

a

b

c

d

e

f

2 Choose the correct words to complete the paragraph.

> show   live performances   elaborate   special effects   actors

I went to a fantastic ¹_____ last week. It was a new musical. The costumes were very ²_____ , and the ³_____ (especially the smoke and the snow) were amazing. I prefer ⁴_____ to TV shows or movies because you really feel the energy from the ⁵_____ ! It was so good. I'd really like to see it again!

3 Find and circle ten words that you have learned.

> show   concert   acrobatics
> sneaker   tragedy   alibi   lighting
> project   opera   comedy

M	J	C	C	N	C	X	W	N	N
A	C	R	O	B	A	T	I	C	S
L	O	P	M	P	S	H	O	W	N
I	N	X	E	R	E	I	P	T	E
B	C	V	D	O	Z	R	V	R	A
I	E	H	Y	J	P	C	A	A	K
P	R	V	K	E	K	G	Y	G	E
A	T	Q	C	C	H	H	A	E	R
L	I	G	H	T	I	N	G	D	J
Y	I	A	P	Q	L	T	J	Y	C

4 Complete the email with the correct form of the verbs in parentheses. Use the present simple for future events.

Grade 7: Field Trip Next Tuesday
Dear Parents,
The 7th grade class is going to the theater to see an Indonesian puppet show next Tuesday.
The bus [1]_____ (leave) at 10:30 a.m. We [2]_____ (arrive) in town for lunch at 12 noon.
The performance [3]_____ (start) at 2 p.m. The bus [4]_____ (leave) the theater at 5:30 p.m., and we [5]_____ (get) back at to school at 7 p.m.
Any questions? Please email me.
Mrs. Turner

FOR ONE DAY ONLY!

See the world-famous Indonesian puppeteers on Tuesday, May 10 at 2 p.m. and 7 p.m. at the City Theater

5 Write questions about the underlined words.

a The dancers arrived at the theater at 3 p.m.

Who _____

b The dancers arrived at the theater at 3 p.m.

_____

c The dancers put on their makeup.

_____

d The dancers put on their beautiful costumes.

_____

e The dancers put on their beautiful costumes at 4 p.m.

_____

6 Complete the sentences with the best conjunction: *and*, *but*, or *so*.

a The theater has just opened, _____ you can buy your tickets now.

b They have sold most of the tickets, _____ there are still a few left.

c I saw the show last night, _____ I know you will enjoy it.

SPEAKING MISSION

1 Choose the correct words to complete the email.

admission fee   events   expensive   festival   program   workshop   schedule

Hi Pip,

Have you seen the information about the music ¹_____? There are lots of different ²_____ over the three days. The ³_____ and the full ⁴_____, including all the times, are on the town website.

I want to take a drumming ⁵_____. It isn't ⁶_____ —I think the ⁷_____ is only $10 for students.

Let's go! I'll call you tomorrow,

Toby

2 Match the questions with the answers.

1 Where is the festival?   a It's in July.
2 When is it?   b Three days.
3 How long does it last?   c It's at Parklands.
4 What can you see there?   d Yes, you do.
5 Do you have to buy tickets?   e Yes, there's a special program for children.
6 Is it entertaining for kids?   f It's an arts festival, so there is a lot to see and do!

3 Answer the questions about the festival you talked about on pages 92 and 93 in the Student's Book.

When is your festival? _____

What can you see at your festival? _____

How much does it cost? _____

Do I have to buy tickets? _____

What can you remember about Unit 4? Do the quiz.

1 What type of show is this?

_____

2 How many hours of practice can a ballet take?

a 50   b 500   c 5,000

_____

3 Where is Wayang Kulit from?

_____

4 What is this?

_____

5 What was the title of the play that this animal was a character in?

_____

6 Complete with the correct form of _leave_.

I've just looked at the website. It says the plane _____ at 9 a.m. tomorrow.

7 Write a question about the underlined word.

<u>Henry</u> solved the crime.

_____

_____

8 Write a question about the underlined word.

Henry solved <u>the crime</u>.

_____

_____

9 Three of these words are similar. Circle the word that is different.

event   program   schedule   timetable

10 Your friend has an idea for a play. You think it's a good idea. What do you say?

a I'm right.   b I agree because …
c You're wrong.   d I disagree because …

Check your answers in the Student's Book. How did you do?

8–10 ☐ Wow!   6–7 ☐ Good job!   0–5 ☐ Try harder!

 ? What makes going to a show so exciting? Write three things.

_____

_____

_____

5 How can we stay healthy?

1 ▶ **5.1** **Watch the video. Complete the graphic organizer. Two items are not needed.**

> bones   muscles   brain
> heart   nervous system
> windpipe   lungs   kidneys
> skin   digestive system

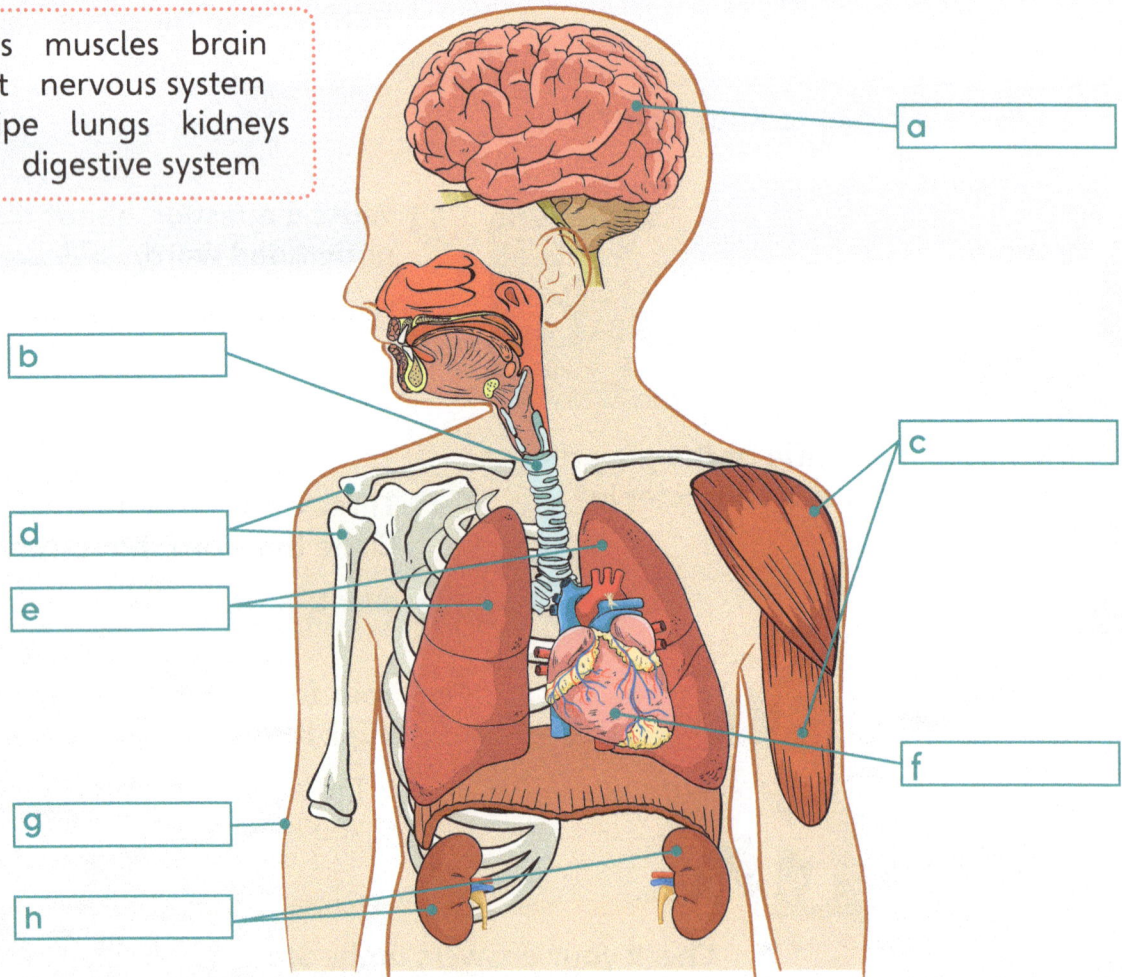

a

b

c

d

e

f

g

h

2 Key Words 1 **Complete the sentences.**

a Your ___nervous system___ , including your _____ , controls your body.

b Your stomach and the rest of your _____ convert your food into nutrients for your body.

c When you breathe, your _____ and _____ take in air.

d Your _____ remove the waste from your body.

e Your _____ and bones work together so that you can move.

Ready to Read: Nonfiction

1 **Key Words 2** **Choose the correct words to complete the crossword.**

> oxygen   blood   cells   systems   chemicals   calories   flexible   nutrients   organs   tissue

Across

1 The things in your food your body needs.
4 There are trillions of these in your body.
6 One of the gases in air.
7 These are the things in food that give us energy.
8 Your heart and kidneys are two of these.
9 If you can touch your toes, you are this.

Down

2 This is made up of the same type of cells.
3 Nervous and digestive
_____.
4 Endorphins are examples of these.
5 The red liquid in your body.

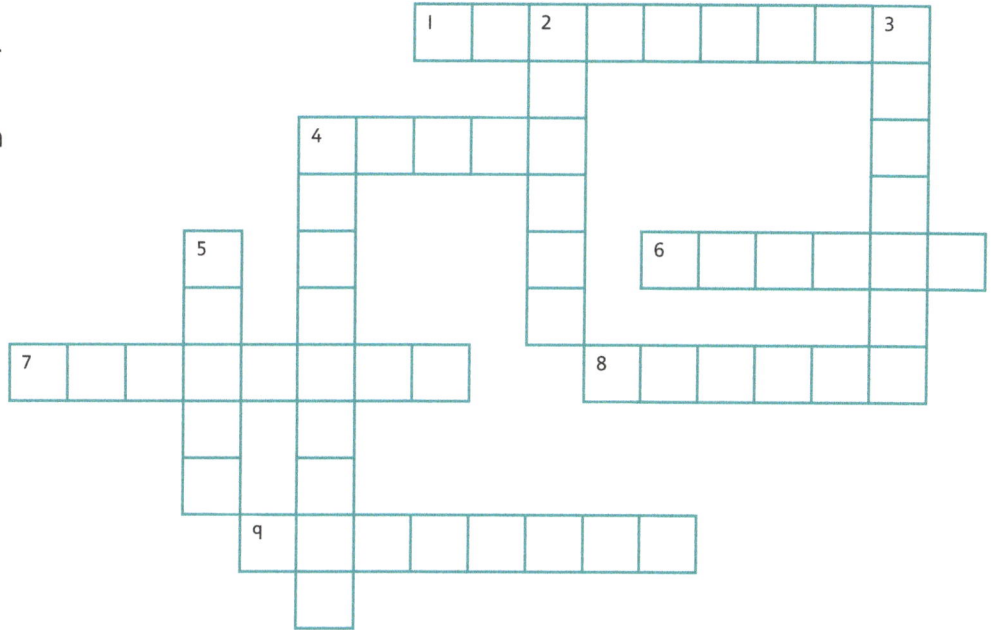

2 **Complete the dialogue with words from the crossword.**

Anna   That was an interesting class, but what a lot of information!

Jack   OK, I'll test you. What are the heart, kidneys, and lungs?

Anna   That's easy: they're all ¹_____!

Jack   Good. What do we take in when we breathe?

Anna   ²_____! OK, now me. What is red and is pumped around our bodies?

Jack   ³_____! OK, diet. What does a good diet have a balance of?

Anna   ⁴_____, I think.

Jack   You're right! Now what are there trillions of in our body?

Anna   ⁵_____. That's easy! Now a question for you. Do you know the name of two systems in our body?

Jack   The ⁶_____ system and the ⁷_____ system!

Anna   Well, I think we know all about the human body now!

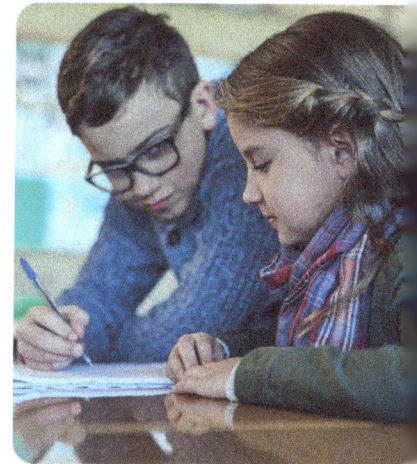

Reading Strategy: Background Knowledge

When we read a text, we can use previous knowledge about the topic and our personal experience to help us understand it.

1 **When do you drink a lot of water? Mark ✓.**

On a hot summer's day? ☐

When you're doing a sport? ☐

Before you do a sport? ☐

In class? ☐

2 **Which of the following sentences applies to you? Mark ✓.**

People say it's important to drink water. I don't know why. ☐

I think I know why we have to drink water, but I'm not 100% sure. Can you tell me? ☐

I know all about sweat, hydration, and dehydration. I can explain it to you. ☐

3 **Read the web page. Why do we have to drink water when we are hot?** _____

| Home | News | Problems | Contact Us | I want to know why … I sweat! 🔍 |

Does your face get red when you have been exercising for a while? Do you feel hot? Is there sweat on your forehead? Have you ever wondered why that happens? Read on and find out!

What do we do when the weather is hot? In the 21st century, we turn on the air conditioning or an electric fan. We know they will help us cool down. But the human body has known how to cool itself down since long before there were electric fans or air-conditioning systems. It has its own cooling system. How does it work?

First, try this experiment. Put a drop of water on the back of your hand, blow on it for a few minutes, and it will disappear—or evaporate. How does the place where the water was feel now? It feels cooler. Why? Because when the water on our skin evaporates, it takes the heat away from that place, and we feel cooler.

Our bodies do something similar. When we exercise and get hot, our blood carries the heat away from our muscles and tissues and distributes it throughout our bodies. The rise in temperature causes the part of our brain that regulates our body temperature to send a signal to the sweat glands in our skin. These glands then produce sweat, which is about 90% water, and it comes out of tiny holes, or pores, in our skin.

Like the drop of water on the back of your hand, the sweat from our pores evaporates and cools the skin. There are between 2 and 4 million sweat glands in the human body. The only places where there are no sweat glands are on our fingernails and toenails, our ears, and our lips.

We sweat all the time, but we sweat a lot more when it's hot and when we are doing physical exercise. When we sweat, we lose a lot of water from our bodies. If we lose too much, we can become dehydrated. In extreme cases, dehydration can be dangerous. It's very important to replace the water that we lose through sweating. If we don't, we might get sick. So always remember to drink lots of water on hot days and when you are exercising.

SB pages 96–99

4 **Read the sentences. Are they true (T) or false (F)?**

a Our bodies can cool themselves down.

b When you blow on water on the back of your hand, the place feels hotter.

c Sweat from our sweat glands evaporates.

d There are sweat glands on all parts of our body.

e We sweat most when it's cold.

f If you drink water when you exercise, you will feel sick.

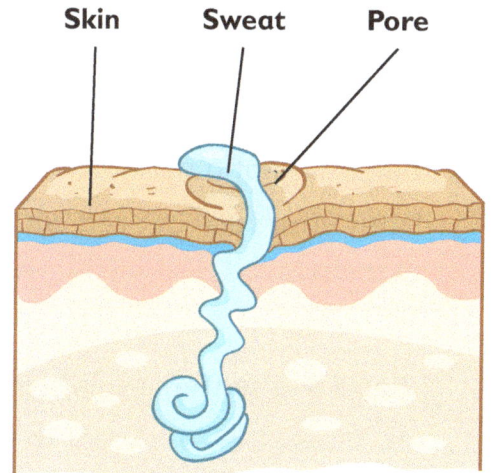

Skin   Sweat   Pore

A Human Sweat Gland

5 **Choose the best title for the article. Mark ✓.**

a Drink Water If You Can

b How Our Body Works: Sweat

c Why Our Skin Is Important

6 **Look at the diagram and answer the questions.**

a How much water should you drink every day? _____

b How much water did you drink today and yesterday? _____

c Was it enough? _____

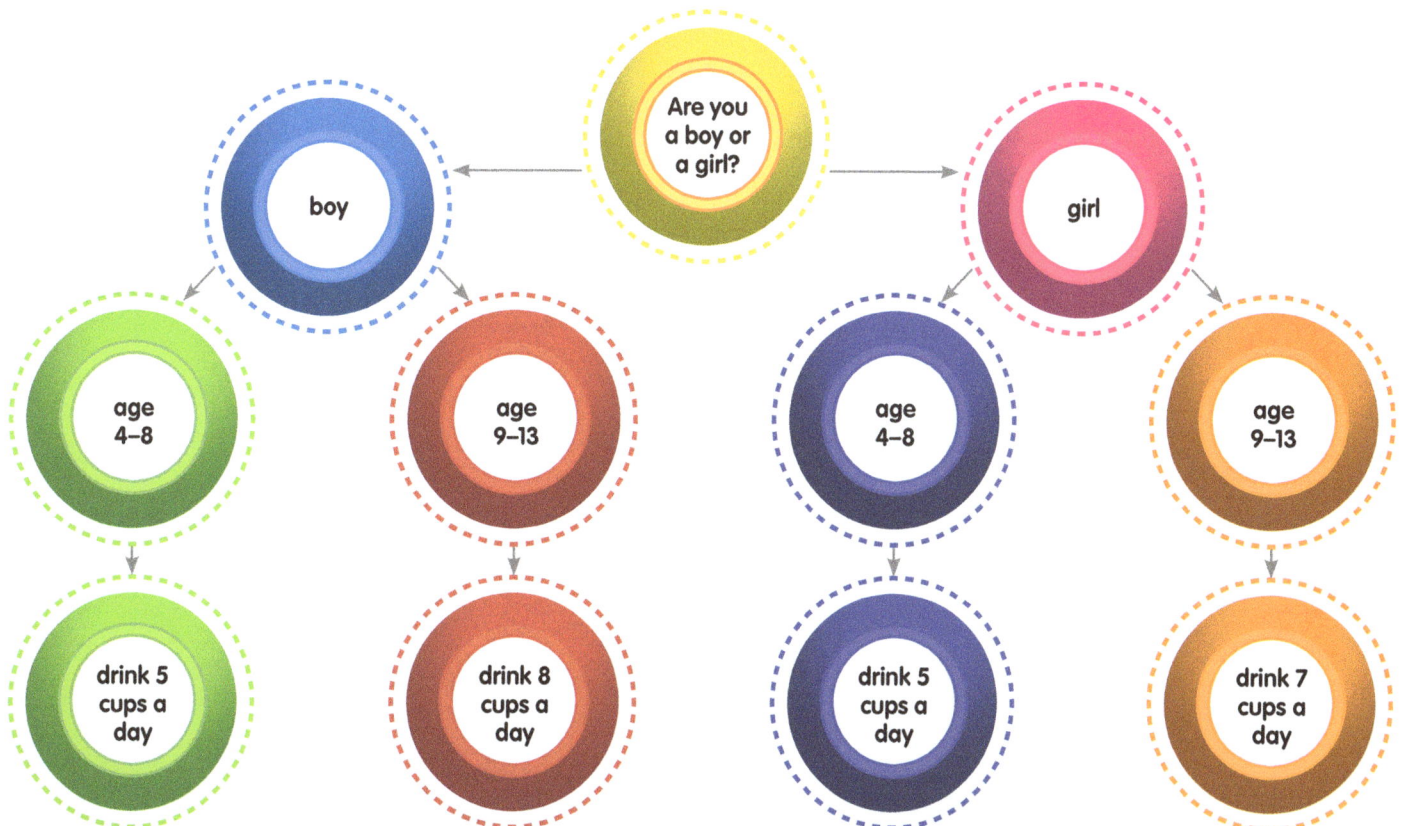

Are you a boy or a girl?

boy

girl

age 4–8

age 9–13

age 4–8

age 9–13

drink 5 cups a day

drink 8 cups a day

drink 5 cups a day

drink 7 cups a day

Present Perfect Progressive

We use the present perfect progressive to describe something we started doing in the past and are still doing now. We use *have been* or *has been* and the *-ing* form of the verb. We can use the present perfect progressive with *for* (a period of time) or *since* (the beginning of a period of time).

Does your face get red when you **have been exercising for** a while?

Our class **has been using** Activity Book 5 **since** the beginning of the school year.

1 **Read the sentences. Which things are still happening now? Mark ✓.**

a I'm so bored! I want to play outside, but it has been raining for hours. ☐

b Mark's face is very red. He has been exercising since 8 a.m.! ☐

c Mom has washed the car. It's clean now. ☐

2 **Complete the sentences with the correct form of the verb in parentheses.**

a My friend ___has been writing___ (write) a story for over an hour.

b I _____ (look) at my social media pages since I finished breakfast.

c The children _____ (watch) some interesting programs on TV this week.

d We _____ (practice) some new dance steps at school this semester.

3 **Look at the pictures. Write sentences using the present progressive form of the verbs in parentheses and *for* or *since*.**

a (paint / 2 o'clock) _____

b (swim / 10:30 this morning) _____

c (play the piano / 3 hours) _____

d (make a cake / an hour) _____

4 **Write sentences using the present perfect progressive and *for* or *since*.**

a Frank went to live in Australia two years ago. He's still living there.

   Frank has been living in Australia for _____ two years.

b The snow started an hour ago. It's still snowing now.

   _____ an hour.

c Timothy and his mom went shopping at 8:30 this morning. They are still at the mall.

   _____ 8:30 this morning.

d Eveline started building a model airplane on May Ist. She hasn't finished it.

   _____ May Ist.

5 **Choose the correct verbs to complete the dialogue. Use the present perfect progressive.**

learn   jump   do x 2   dance   go   run   work out   go

Alexandra Your face is very red, Bruno! What ¹ have you been doing?

Bruno I ² _____ at the gym with an instructor.

Alexandra What ³ _____ to do?

Bruno Lots of new things. Today, I ⁴ _____ on the treadmill. I go to the gym twice a week. I'm trying to do a lot of aerobic activity.

Alexandra What else ⁵ _____ ?

Bruno I ⁶ _____ . I go to a really great hip-hop class!

Alexandra That sounds like fun!

Bruno But what about you, Alex? What have you been up to?

Alexandra Lots of things! I ⁷ _____ to the gym, too. And I ⁸ _____ rope. It's great exercise.

My Life

Read and answer the questions.

What have you been reading? _____

What have you been practicing? _____

What have you been learning? _____

Spelling Patterns and Word Study

1 **Look at the pictures and write the words. They all have the same sound.**

> hair   bear   stare

a

b

c

_____   _____   _____

2 **Complete the sentences with a word ending in *-ear*, *-are*, or *-air*.**

a We can sh ___ ___ ___ the colored pencils.

b Do you like fruit? Would you like a p ___ ___ ___ ?

c The table is broken. Let's rep ___ ___ ___ it.

d I want to w ___ ___ ___ my red dress today.

e Please shut the window. Too much cold ___ ___ ___ is coming in!

f Do you agree? I really c ___ ___ ___ what you think.

Oracy

> Trampolining is awesome.

> And it's good exercise, too!

1 **Which fun activity to make a sad friend feel better did you talk about in Oracy Time?**

My fun activity was _____ .

2 **Which fun activity did your partner talk about?**

My partner's fun activity was _____ .

3 **How did you give your partner encouragement? What did you say? What did you do?**

This is what I said:

_____

This is what I did:

_____

Improve Your Writing

Parallel Structure

We use parallel structure to make sentences easier to read. Parallel structure means using the same grammar pattern, for example, in lists, which often have words like *and*, *but*, and *or*. We can use only verbs in the same form or only nouns, only adjectives, or only adverbs.

Parallel	Not Parallel
The children like swimming, running, and sailing. (all *-ing* forms) **My dad likes concerts, musicals, and live performances.** (all nouns)	**The children like swimming, to run, and sailboats.** (*-ing* form, *to* verb, noun) **My dad likes going to concerts, musicals, and watching live performances.** (*-ing* form + noun, noun, *-ing* form + noun)

1 **Read and label the sentences *P* (parallel structure) or *NP* (not parallel structure).**

a Eating healthy foods helps you feel healthier, good, and stronger. ☐

b Vegetables, fruit, and cereals give us plenty of fiber. ☐

c You should try to eat slowly, to be careful, and having small portions. ☐

d For breakfast, I eat yogurt, fruit, and cereal. ☐

2 **Rewrite the sentences to give them parallel structure.**

a Margot spent the weekend doing her homework, playing tennis, and she went to the café.

_____

b I can relax by having a cup of tea or if I take a quick brain break.

_____

c That store is a good place for vegetables, meat, and to buy fruit.

_____

3 **Complete the sentences with a parallel structure.**

a Before his run, Steve put on his sneakers and _____ and picked up his
_____.

b My mom can draw, paint, and _____
_____.

c I'd love to go to a movie, the zoo, or _____
_____.

d My friend likes playing tennis, riding her bike, and _____
_____.

Writing

1 READ Choose the correct words to complete the paragraph. Then, underline one example of parallel structure in the paragraph.

five   nose   quiet   smell   smile   work

A brain break gives your brain a quick, 1_____-minute rest. You should do it somewhere 2_____ —you don't want noise! When you start, try to breathe in and out through your 3_____. Relax your eyes, keep your mouth closed, and imagine a calm place, like the ocean. As you imagine the ocean, you can use your senses— sight, touch, sound, and 4_____. 5_____ gently to yourself at the same time. Brain breaks are a good way to relax for a short time. Your 6_____ will be better after you've had one!

2 PLAN You are going to write an instructional text using some parallel structures. Use one of these ideas or your own. Make notes in the graphic organizer.

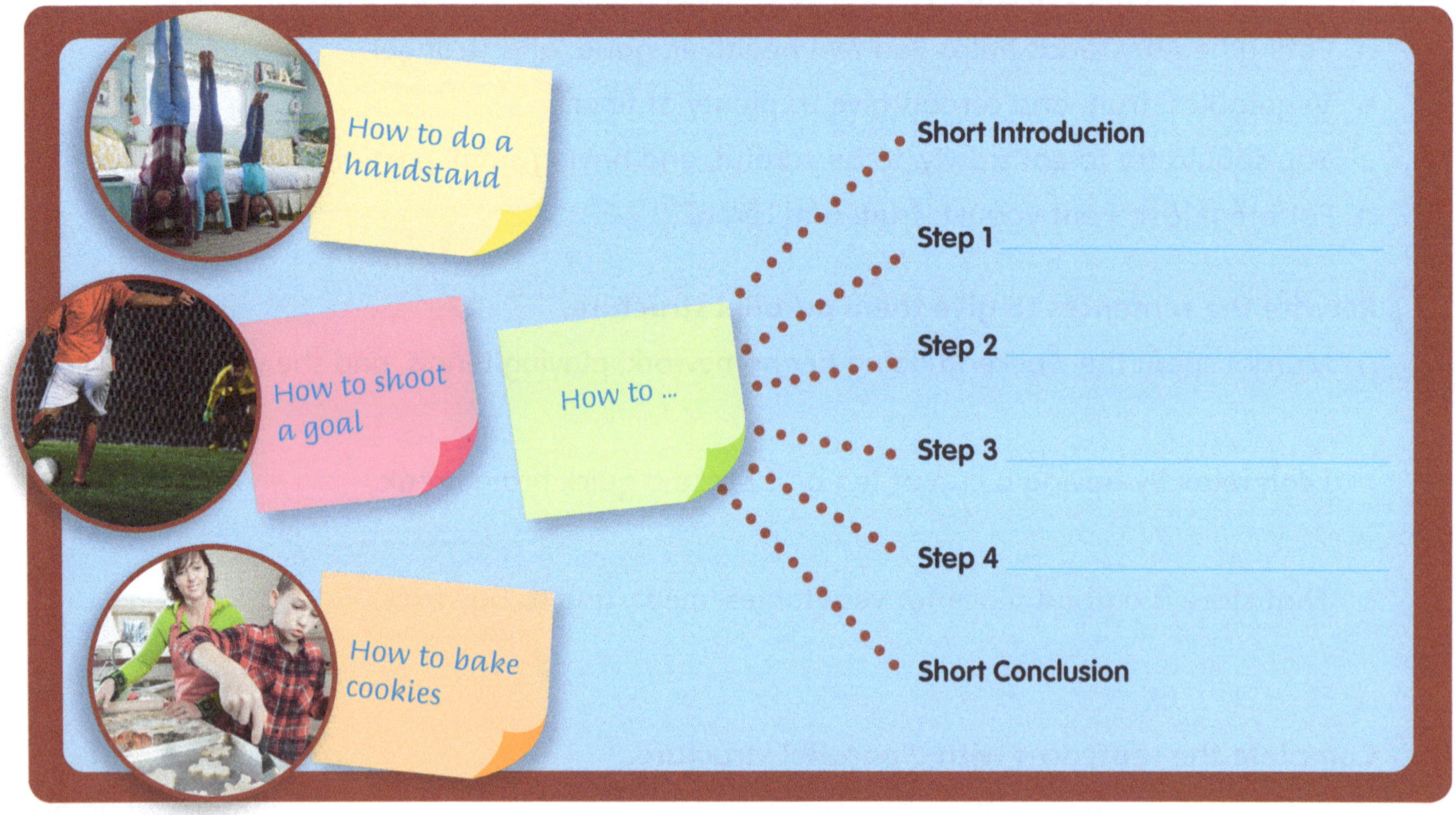

How to do a handstand

How to shoot a goal

How to ...

How to bake cookies

Short Introduction

Step 1 _____

Step 2 _____

Step 3 _____

Step 4 _____

Short Conclusion

3 WRITE Use your notes to write your instructional text.

4 EDIT Read your work and mark ✓.

Did you:

- include a title? ☐
- use all your notes? ☐
- include parallel structure? ☐

Ready to Read: Fiction

1 **Key Words 4** **Look at the pictures and write the words.**

field   jumping jacks   pass   push-ups   striker   red card

a

b

c

d

e

f

2 **Circle the correct word to complete the sentences.**

a The soccer **season / defenders** in the U.S.A. starts in March.

b **Defenders / Midfielders** try to stop the other team from scoring a goal.

c If a player kicks another player deliberately, it is a **foul / tackle**.

d If a player wants to get the ball from another player, he or she **strikes / tackles**.

e If a player gets a **red / yellow** card, he or she must leave the game immediately.

f **Strikers / Midfielders** play mainly in the central part of the field.

3 **Answer the questions.**

a How many **push-ups** can you do? _____

b How many **jumping jacks** can you do? _____

c Which **position** in soccer would you like to play/do you play? _____

Reading Strategy: Making Inferences

Inferences are guesses that we make about what an author wants to say. We combine clues from the text with our knowledge and experience to make inferences.

1 Read the first paragraph. Answer the questions and complete the table

	Clue in the Text	My Knowledge or Experience	My Inference
a What time of day was it?	+	=	
b What did Jason do when he arrived home? Why?	+	=	

The Park Run

Jason arrived home from school just before dark, and he sat down at the kitchen table. His mom asked him about his day, but he wasn't really listening. He was thinking about all the homework he had to do. Final exams were starting in six weeks, and he was worried.

"What's the matter?" his mom asked. "You've been staring at your plate for the last ten minutes, but you haven't eaten anything!"

Jason let out a moan and said, "Mom, I can't eat. I feel sick."

He told his mom about the homework and his worries about his final exams. "I have so much to do," he said. "I wish I had more time."

"OK," she said. "This is stress. It's not good for you, so we're going to do something about it. You've been studying too much. It's time for bed now, but we'll start tomorrow."

The next day, they went to the park. It was busy. One group of children was doing jumping jacks, another group was kicking a ball, and another group was carrying rackets and balls.

"Mom, what are we doing here?" Jason complained. "You know I hate soccer!"

"We're going to run in the park!"

So, they ran five kilometers together, and Jason ran like the wind! At the end, they were sweating, but they were also smiling.

"Well, now that we've done some aerobic exercise," Jason's mom said, "let's do some relaxation exercises."

They joined a group that was sitting on blankets on the grass. The instructor told them to close their eyes and imagine they were walking on a beautiful beach. At the end of the relaxation, Jason felt very calm.

After that, Jason and his mom went home and ate a salad for lunch.

"I feel really great!" said Jason. "But why?"

His mom explained that it was important to take care of yourself and not just study. She told him he needed to exercise, eat healthy food, and do relaxation exercises every day.

"You'll feel better and happier," she said. "But, most importantly, always tell me when you're feeling worried."

"Thanks, Mom, you're the best!" said Jason, smiling.

For the next six weeks, Jason followed his mom's advice, and he got the highest grades in his class on all of his final exams.

SB pages 105–10

2 **Read the whole story. Put the pictures in the correct order.**

a
☐

b
☐

c
☐

d
☐

3 **Read the story again. Circle the correct words to complete the sentences.**

a Jason was worried about his **soccer game / his homework**.

b His mom noticed he wasn't **eating his dinner / doing his homework**.

c The next day the park was very **busy / quiet**.

d After the relaxation exercise, Jason felt **stressed / relaxed**.

e His mom explained t**he importance / the meaning** of looking after his body and his mind.

f At the end of the story, Jason felt much **better / worse** than at the beginning.

4 **Answer the questions and complete the table.**

	Clue in the Text	My Knowledge or Experience	My Inference
What activities were happening in the park?		+	=
Why do you think Jason got his best grades ever?		+	=

5 **Is there a park near your home? What activities can you do there to exercise your body and mind?**

Statements with *wish*

We use *wish* to describe things we want to be different from how they are at the moment. We use the past simple after *wish*, but we are talking about the present, not the past.

I wish I had more time. (Jason doesn't have much time.)

I wish I didn't have so much homework. (Jason has a lot of homework.)

1 **Circle the correct form of the verb to complete the sentences.**

a I wish I **can / could** play rugby.

b I wish I **live / lived** in a bigger house.

c I wish I **am / was** rich.

d I wish I **have / had** a pet rabbit.

2 **Complete the sentences with the correct forms of the verbs in parentheses.**

a I wish I _____ (can / do) more push-ups. I can only do four.

b I wish we _____ (not / have) a test tomorrow. I don't like tests!

c I wish I _____ (live) closer to the mountains. I love climbing.

d I wish we _____ (can / go) to a theme park today, but my sister wants to go shopping. Boring!

e I wish these exercises _____ (not / be) so hard. I'd like to do something different.

3 **Look at the pictures. What do the people wish? Complete the sentences. Use the correct form of the verbs in parentheses.**

a

b

c

d

I wish I _____   I wish I _____   I wish I _____   I wish I _____

_____   _____   _____   _____

_____   _____   _____   _____

_____ (be).   _____ (live in Australia).   _____ (have).   _____ (can play).

94

4 Read about these situations. What could you say?

a Your laptop doesn't work.

b You don't live close to your school.

c It's raining. You don't have your umbrella.

d You are at a party. Everyone is having fun. They can dance, but you can't.

5 Look at the song on page III in the Student's Book. Who do you wish you were? Think of a friend. What can they do that you can't? What do they have that you don't? Write your own verse for the song. Try to make it rhyme!

I wish I could _____

like _____ .

_____

I wish I _____

_____ .

and _____

_____ .

My Life

Complete the sentences so that they are true for you.

I wish I had _____ .

I wish I lived _____ .

I wish I could _____ .

I wish I was _____ .

Values: Keeping Physically and Mentally Healthy

1 Think back to the story *The Park Run* on page 92 and answer the questions.

a What did Jason do to be physically healthy?

_____

b What did he do to be mentally healthy?

_____

c How did Jason feel at the end of the story? Why?

_____

2 Look at the activities. Decide if they can help you to keep physically or mentally healthy or both. Mark ✓.

	To Keep Physically Healthy	To Keep Mentally Healthy
go for a run		
take a brain break when you are studying		
eat fruit		
get a good night's sleep		
do yoga		
join a gym and do regular exercise		
play outside		
drink water		
leave your cell phone in the kitchen at night		

3 Can you add two more ideas to the table above?

4 Answer the questions for yourself.

What activities do you do to keep physically healthy?

_____

What activities do you do to keep mentally healthy?

_____

Check Your Oracy: Giving Encouragement

1	I tried to sound interested.	All the time / Most of the time / Sometimes
2	I gave my partner encouragement.	All the time / Most of the time / Sometimes
3	I used the phrases on the cue cards.	All of them / Most of them / Some of them

The Big Challenge STEAM: Science & Math

How can we create a class fitness program?

a **Which day of the week did you make a plan for? What was the exercise for the day? What was the relaxation?**

_____

b **How well did you do? Color the stars to give yourself a score.***

I made three lists: healthy foods, physical activities, and relaxation activities.	☆☆☆☆☆
I made a plan for my day.	☆☆☆☆☆
I presented the plan for my day to the class.	☆☆☆☆☆

*(5 = Awesome! 4 = Pretty good, 3 = OK, 2 = Could be better, 1 = Needs more work!)

c **Which other plan did you like the best?**

_____

d **What could you do better next time?**

_____

The Big Question and **Me**

Because of the things I have learned in this unit,

I will _____

_____

1 **Look at the pictures and write the words.**

muscles   heart   bone   brain   lungs   kidneys

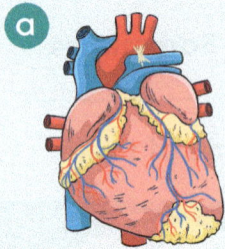

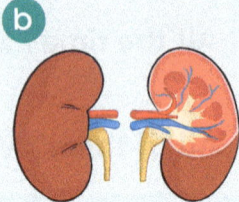

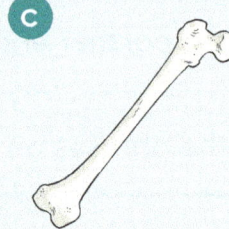

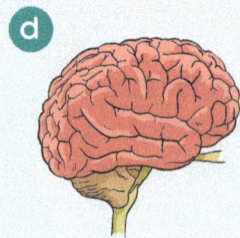

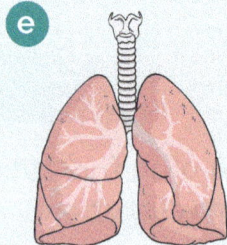

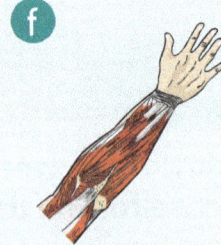

a _____

b _____

c _____

d _____

e _____

f _____

2 **Match the words with the definitions.**

1 flexible

2 aerobic

3 pump

4 calories

5 oxygen

6 windpipe

a Your heart does this with the blood in your body.

b We measure the energy in food in these.

c If your muscles are this, you can touch your toes.

d This connects your nose and mouth to your lungs.

e Running and riding a bike are this type of exercise.

f This is in the air. Plants and animals need it to live.

3 **Choose the correct words to complete the paragraph.**

field   foul   injuries   passes   striker   red card

And welcome back to this exciting game. Out on the
[1] _____, both teams are playing well. Number 8
[2] _____ the ball to number 9—number 9 is our
[3] _____. Is he going to score a goal? Oh, no!
What's happening now? The referee is holding up a
[4] _____. There has been a [5] _____,
but who committed it? Was it number 9 from the blue
team … or number 10 from the red team?
Both players are holding their legs. Are there
any serious [6] _____? No, both
players are OK.

4 Look at the pictures. What have they been doing? Write sentences.

a
(fix)

_____

b
(climb)

_____

c
(eat)

_____

d
(shop)

_____

_____

5 Write sentences with these words and _I_. Use the correct form of the verbs.

a wish / have / a better tablet _____

b wish / live / Canada _____

c wish / be / good at sports _____

d wish / can / meet a famous person _____

6 Rewrite these sentences using parallel structure.

a While we were in the U.S.A., we visited a famous theme park, eating in diners, and took photos of amazing places.

_____

b My aunt decided to paint her office, to buy some new furniture, and that the rug needs to be cleaned.

_____

c Leonardo da Vinci was an inventor, a sculptor, and he painted things.

_____

d My teacher plans lessons, grading homework, and to go to important meetings.

_____

SPEAKING MISSION

1 Look at the pictures and write the verbs.

bake   chop   cut   drain   mix   peel   slice   wash

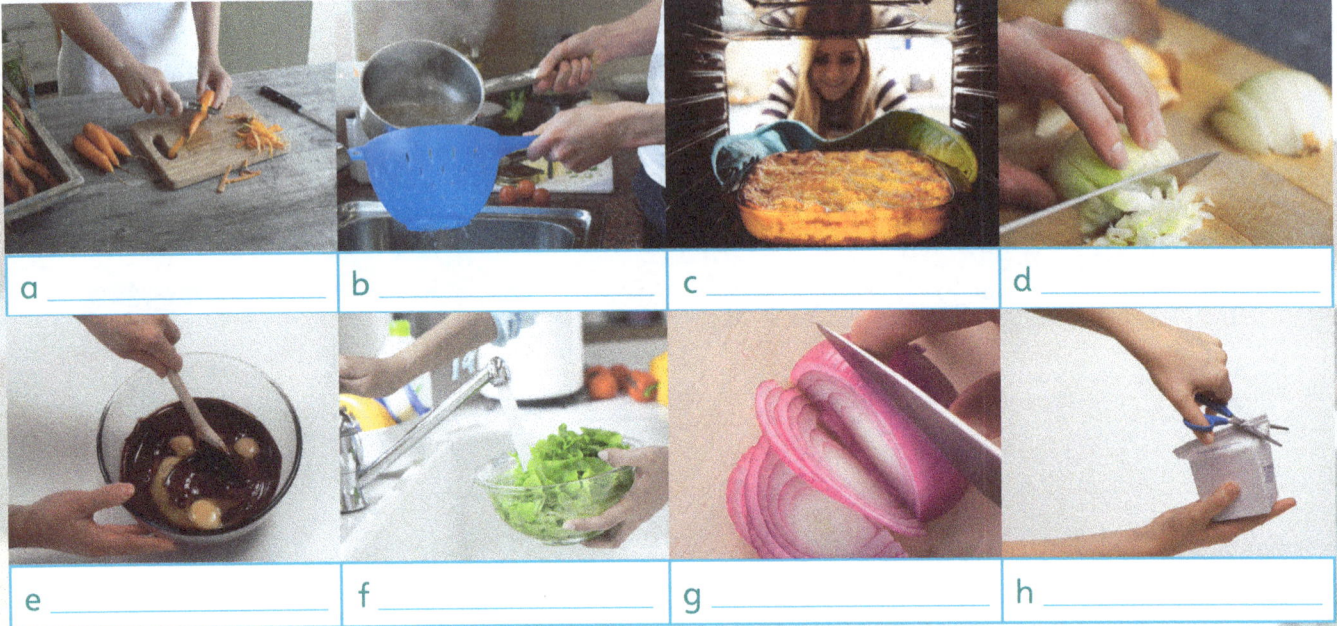

a _____

b _____

c _____

d _____

e _____

f _____

g _____

h _____

2 What does Joe say to Dan? Put the dialogue in the correct order.

Dan   What are we going to make?

Joe   ¹ __b__

Dan   OK. What do we need?

Joe   ² _____

Dan   Do we need anything else?

Joe   ³ _____

Dan   How do we make it?

Joe   ⁴ _____

Dan   That's easy!

Joe   ⁵ _____

Dan   Good idea!

a   OK, first, we chop the garlic. Then, we mix the chickpeas, olive oil, and lemon juice.

b   Let's make hummus. It's easy, and it's healthy!

c   Oh, yes! Some lemon juice.

d   Chickpeas, olive oil, and some garlic.

e   But we have to mix it a lot! It has to be smooth. Let's use a machine!

3 What is your favorite food? Can you make it?

_____

_____

What can you remember about Unit 5? Do the quiz.

1 Which of these is *not* a healthy habit?

a going to bed early

b eating a big plate of French fries

c playing outside

2 Where can you find healthy fat?

a in avocados b in milk c in meat

3 During aerobic exercise, do you breathe faster or more slowly?

_____

4 How long does a brain break take?

a 10 minutes b 30 minutes c 5 minutes

5 What did the boys in *Finding Your Wings* use to make the rules for the training program?

a a book b a video game c an app

6 What are these?

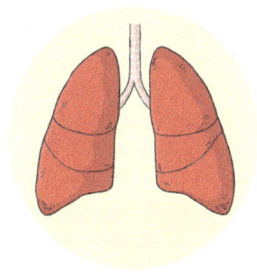

_____

7 What is the boy thinking?

I wish I

_____

soccer better.

8 Complete the sentence with the present perfect progressive form of *play*.

I'm tired! I _____ basketball for nearly two hours!

9 What is this?

It's a _____.

10 Complete the sentence.

Some easy exercises are short runs, push-ups, and

_____

_____.

Check your answers in the Student's Book. How did you do?

8–10 ☐ Wow!   6–7 ☐ Good job!   0–5 ☐ Try harder!

? 😊 **How can we stay healthy?** Write three things.

_____

_____

_____

6 Why is language special?

1 ▶ 6.1 **Watch the video. Complete the graphic organizer.**

> cooperate with people   learn from the past   share different and interesting ideas
> solve complex problems   understand other cultures

Human Communication

Causes	Effects
a Human language has a huge variety of words and meanings.	We can _____ _____ .
b Humans can talk about abstract ideas.	We can understand and _____ _____ .
c Language allows us to negotiate and reach agreement with other people.	We can _____ _____ outside our own family or community.
d Human language is passed down to future generations.	We can _____ _____ .
e We learn different languages.	We can _____ _____ .

2 Key Words 1 **Match the words with the definitions.**

1 unique
2 abstract
3 complex
4 cooperate
5 negotiate

a (*verb*) to work together

b (*adjective*) involving a lot of different but related parts in a way that is difficult to understand

c (*adjective*) relating to ideas and not real things

d (*verb*) to try to reach an agreement about something by discussing it

e (*adjective*) different from every other person or thing

SB pages 116–17

Ready to Read: Nonfiction

1 Key Words 2 **Look at the pictures. Write the words.**

shapes   alphabet   emoji   hieroglyphics   symbol

a   b   c   d   e

_____   _____   _____   _____   _____

2 **Choose the correct words to complete the sentences.**

bilingual   common   formal   minority   native speakers

a   Mandarin has more _____ than any other language.

b   The country with the greatest number of _____ languages is Papua New Guinea.

c   An example of _____ writing is a business letter.

d   If you speak two languages, you are _____.

e   The most _____ alphabet is the Roman alphabet.

3 **Choose the correct words to complete the paragraph.**

emojis   formal   hieroglyphics   shapes

Written Language: A Project by Bernardo Rosa

The Ancient Egyptians had one of the oldest ways of recording language. They used
[1]_____: pictures and [2]_____ that had meanings. They started to use
this system around 5,000 years ago. Over the centuries, as more people needed to write,
written languages became more complex and [3]_____. However, in the 21st
century, because we now communicate by texting and emailing, our writing is becoming
more informal again, and we use [4]_____ a lot.

1 **Read the blog. Match the numbers with the facts.**

1 7,000   **a** a historical event in the U.S.A.

2 2,000   **b** the number of Native American languages that are still spoken in California

3 2016   **c** the number of minority languages in the world with 1,000 speakers or fewer

4 1848   **d** the number of languages in the world

5 50   **e** when the last speaker of Wichita died

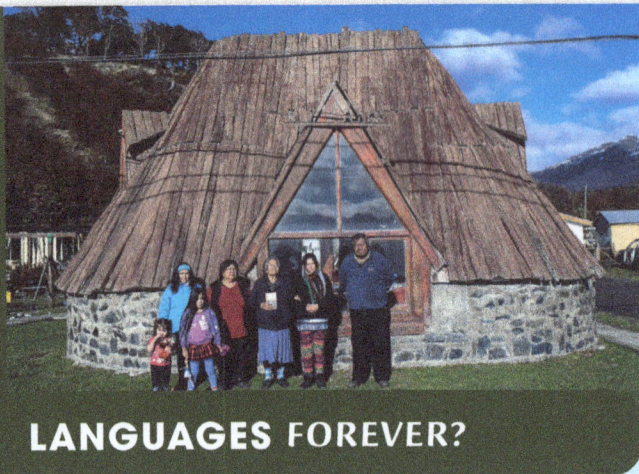

LANGUAGES FOREVER?

The other day, I came across this photo of a family in front of their house in Chile. Nothing special, right? Wrong! The old woman in the middle is the last speaker of her native language, Yagan. It got me thinking about disappearing languages.

Are Languages Disappearing?

Did you know that according to UNESCO (the United Nations Educational, Scientific, and Cultural Organization) there are about 7,000 languages in the world today? However, many of these are described as "minority languages." A recent report said that more than 2,000 of these minority languages had 1,000 or fewer speakers. They also said that 90% of Native American languages are not passed on to the next generation. At the time of the California Gold Rush (1848), there were around 100 Native American languages in California. Today there are only 50. The last speaker of Wichita, one of the native languages of Oklahoma, died in 2016. These are all examples of minority languages. I believe that the disappearance of these languages is a tragedy.

Why Do Languages Disappear?

I wanted to know how a language just disappears! I learned that, in 2014, the University of Cambridge published a report on exactly this question. It said that there are many complex reasons languages disappear, but an important one relates to economic growth. People move from the country to the city to earn more money and give their children a better education. Children who are born in the city grow up speaking the language of the city, which may be different from the language of their parents and grandparents. And so that language is forgotten.

What Is Lost When a Language Disappears?

To me, language is more than words. A society's language is also its culture. People use their language to organize their society and to build relationships with each other. When parents don't talk to their children in their native language, the link between those children and previous generations is broken. When a language disappears, a society's culture, traditions, and history are lost forever.

What About the Future?

There are now projects in many parts of the world that are trying to keep minority languages alive, and some governments have passed laws to keep them safe. For example, in Wales in the U.K., the minority language, Welsh, is an official language. Similar changes are happening in other countries. Did you know that Spain now has five official languages? Spanish covers the whole country, but Catalonia, Aragon, Galicia, and the Basque region now have their own official languages as well. I hope that fewer languages will disappear in the future.

How can we make sure minority languages don't disappear? Post your comments.

2 **Read the blog again. Label the sentences _T_ (true) or _F_ (false).**

    a There are about 10,000 different languages in the world. ☐

    b Over 2,000 of the 7,000 languages spoken in the world today have 1,000 or fewer speakers. ☐

    c There are the same number of Native American languages in California today as there were in 1848. ☐

    d There is no one alive now who is a native speaker of the Wichita language. ☐

    e Economic growth is one of the reasons languages disappear. ☐

    f When a language disappears, the traditions and culture of that society may also disappear. ☐

A Stop Sign Written in Inuktitut, an Inuit Language in Northern Canada.

Reading Strategy: Fact and Opinion

A fact is something that is true for everyone. An opinion is what a person feels or believes about something.

3 **Read the sentences from the blog. Write _F_ (fact) or _O_ (opinion).**

    a There are about 7,000 languages in the world today. ☐

    b 90% of Native American languages are not passed on to the next generation. ☐

    c I believe that the disappearance of these languages is a tragedy. ☐

    d To me, language is more than words. ☐

    e I hope that fewer languages will disappear in the future. ☐

4 **The blogger invites your comments on the final question in her blog. What would you write?**

We can make recordings of people speaking the language.

Reported Statements with *said* and *told*

We can use *said* or *told* to report what someone said. We usually change the verb tense and the pronouns. When we use *told*, we need an object. The use of *that* is optional. We use quotation marks around direct speech, but not around reported speech.

"More than 2,000 minority languages have 1,000 or fewer speakers," the report said.

The report said (that) more than 2,000 minority languages had 1,000 or fewer speakers.

"I'm losing my native language," she told us.

She told us (that) she was losing her native language.

1 Complete the table. Then, circle the correct words in the rule and complete it.

I like ice cream!

Original Tense	Original Speech	Reported Speech
Present Simple	"I like ice cream," said Thomas.	Thomas said ¹_____.
	"My mom ²_____ a red car," said Thomas.	Thomas said his mom drove a red car.

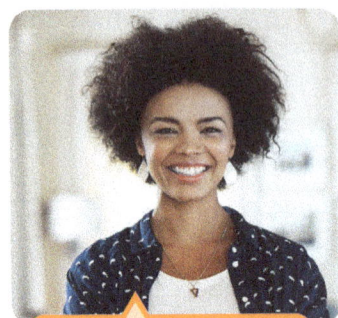

Jason is playing soccer outside.

Original Tense	Original Speech	Reported Speech
Present Progressive	"Jason is playing soccer outside," said Judy.	Judy said Jason ³_____ soccer outside.
	⁴"_____ the new TV show," said Judy.	Judy said she was enjoying the new TV show.

Rule
When we report statements the verb tenses usually **change / stay the same**, for example, from present simple to _____.

2 Complete the sentences with *said* or *told*.

a The children _____ they were cold.

b Our teacher _____ us that she spoke four languages.

c My grandfather _____ it was important to speak clearly.

d My dad _____ me that he wanted to eat Japanese food.

3 Report what the people say.

a "I like the photos," said the girl.

   The girl said she liked the photos. _____

b "I have lots of homework, Mom," Tom said.

   Tom told his mother _____.

c "I want to learn to ride a horse," said Freddie.

   Freddie said _____.

d "I'm making dinner," said Rachel.

   Rachel said _____.

e "We're enjoying the book," said Nick and James.

   Nick and James told their teacher _____.

4 Complete the sentences with the correct pronouns for the reported speech.

a "I like learning languages."

   Michael said ___he___ liked learning languages.

b "We play basketball on Saturdays."

   Johnny and Franklin told me that _____ played basketball on Saturdays.

c "My dad is Japanese."

   Stephanie told me that _____ dad was Japanese.

d "I love my hamster."

   Toby told me that he loved _____ hamster.

My Life

Write two sentences you heard today. Then, report them.

" _____ "

My brother said _____.

" _____ "

My mom told me _____.

Spelling Patterns and Word Study

1 Look at the pictures and write the words. They all have the same long *u* sound.

a gl _ _ _

b fl _ _ _ _ _

c v _ _ _ _ _

2 Read the three words under each picture. Circle the word that has the long *u* sound.

tube   brush   teeth

red   jewel   expensive

meat   dinner   barbecue

car   new   fast

yellow   eight   cube

blue   paint   pot

Oracy

1 Which topic did you and your partner talk about in Oracy Time? Mark ✓.

⭐ **Oracy Time!**

English is the most important language in the world. ☐

Learning another language is not important. ☐

2 Did you agree or disagree with the topic? Mark ✓.

I agreed. ☐   I disagreed. ☐

3 What evidence did you use to support your argument? Write two things you said.

_____

_____

Connecting Words

We can use these words to connect our ideas.

In addition = **and**

However = **but**

Therefore = **so**

We use a comma after these words.

In addition, I speak Spanish.

1 **Read the text and circle the correct connecting words.**

Did you know that people who live in Wales often speak more than one language? Almost everyone speaks English. [1] **Therefore / In addition,** they might speak Welsh. There are many people who speak Welsh. [2] **However / In addition,** monolingual speakers of Welsh are not very common. Almost all children have Welsh lessons at school up to the age of 16. [3] **However / Therefore,** most children understand some Welsh.

2 **Complete the sentences with the best connecting words (*Therefore*, *In addition*, *However*).**

a My parents speak Japanese. _____, my dad speaks French.

b It's easy for children to learn a new language. _____, it can take quite a long time.

c Classes only take place Monday through Friday. _____, children don't have classes on weekends.

d The test doesn't start till 10 a.m. _____, the teacher wants us to be there by 9:30 a.m.

e One of our teachers can teach Chinese. _____, you can learn Chinese at our school with her.

f My friend speaks German and English. _____, he speaks a little Dutch.

Writing

1 READ Look at the text on page 125 in the Student's Book. Match the sentence halves.

1 Sign language is often used

2 In the world there are more than

3 There are grammar rules

4 British Sign Language is completely different

5 The number of people who sign is

a from American Sign Language.

b for each sign language.

c over 70 million.

d when people can't hear.

e 130 unique sign languages.

2 PLAN You are going to write an informational report about learning a language in your school. Make notes in the graphic organizer.

Paragraph 1 Introduction Explain the topic to the reader.

Paragraph 2 Key Fact Why do students learn this language?

Paragraph 3 Key Fact How do students learn this language?

Paragraph 4 Key Fact What is difficult/easy about this language?

Paragraph 5 Conclusion Mention a fact about the language and say something to the reader.

3 WRITE Use your notes to write your informational report.

4 EDIT Read your work and mark ✓.

Did you:

• include the five parts from your notes? ☐

• organize the key facts into paragraphs? ☐

• include connecting words? ☐

1 Key Words 4 **Choose the correct words to complete the sentences.**

> abandon   crave   drawn   inhabit   legally

a _____ , the school has to test the fire alarm every week.

b I was _____ to the lion's cage by the sounds of his roar.

c Komodo dragons _____ some volcanic islands in Indonesia.

d After the tsunami, the people had to _____ their village and go to live in the city.

e Most young children _____ affection.

2 **Choose the correct words to complete the crossword.**

> origin   rumor   myth   mysterious   distant

Across

4 strange and unknown or not understood

5 a very old story from history that people don't think is true

Down

1 something people talk about a lot but don't know if it's true

2 far away in space or time

3 where something begins or comes from

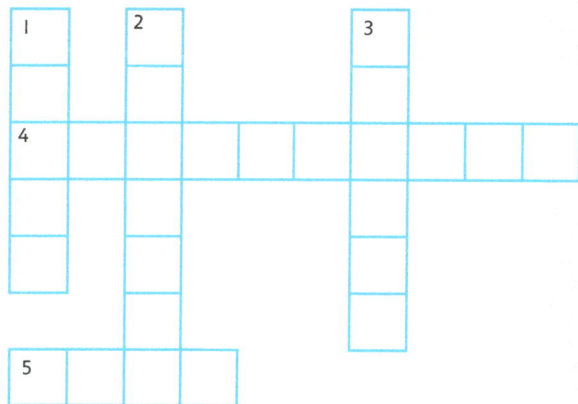

3 **Answer these questions.**

a Name an animal that **inhabits** the ocean. _____

b What food do you **crave** most often? _____

c What kinds of movies are you **drawn** to? _____

d What is your favorite **myth**? _____

1 **Read the story. Which pictures are in the story? Mark ✓.**

a b c d e

The Message

Zahara and her cousin Amir were wandering home after school.

"I really enjoyed our history class today," Zahara said. "It was fun to learn about Egyptian hieroglyphics. I can't wait for the next class because Mrs. Peters told us we could try to decipher some. I'm really drawn to them." She paused and said, "I think I'm going to do my history project on hieroglyphics in Ancient Egypt. What are you going to do?" she asked.

"I have absolutely no idea," said Amir. "But tonight we have to do that math homework!"

"I know," said Zahara, who found math difficult.

"Call me if you need help. Remember the signs," Amir said in a mysterious voice as he walked up his driveway.

"Wait … ," shouted Zahara, but Amir didn't hear her.

She took out her phone and put on her favorite music. "I wonder what Amir meant when he said 'Remember the signs'?" she asked herself.

At home in her bedroom, Zahara opened her math book and began the exercises. "I wish this was history homework!" she thought to herself. Her phone beeped, and she picked it up.

"Whoa!" she thought. "What's this?"

She immediately called Amir.

"Hey, I just got this completely weird mess …"

"A weird message? Me, too!" said Amir at the same time. "Someone told me about this at school. It's a secret code."

"But what does it say?" Zahara asked. "Can you understand it? Who sent it?"

"No, but … wait …. I just got another message … It says HELLO!"

And here's the rest of the message."

"Do you understand the message?" Zahara asked. "If we look at … ," she continued excitedly.

"Yes," Amir replied. "Let's see who can decipher it first! Talk to you soon! Bye!"

Zahara quickly worked out what the message said. She loved codes and puzzles.

"Now I get it!" she thought.

She took a photo and sent it to Amir. At the exact moment the message left her phone, there was a knock at her front door.

"Who can that be?" she wondered, smiling to herself.

"Surprise!" Amir said. "Well done! You worked out my message."

"And now we're going to do the math homework!" Zahara laughed.

"I thought, if you can work out the code, you can work out the math!" Amir said. "And I've come to help you!"

Let's do our homework together!

2 **Read the story again. Label the sentences *T* (true) or *F* (false).**

a At the beginning, Zahara is happy about doing her math homework. ☐

b She listened to some music on her way home. ☐

c Zahara began to do her history homework. ☐

d Zahara enjoyed working out the message. ☐

e Amir wanted Zahara to think math was fun. ☐

> **Reading Strategy:** Analyzing Plot
>
> Plot is the sequence of events within a story. Stories generally have a problem in the middle that the characters have to solve by the end.

3 **Complete the plot diagram about the story with these sentences.**

Zahara received a text message in hieroglyphics.

The children did their math homework together.

Zahara worked out the meaning of the code.

The children walked home from school.

Zahara understood her cousin was helping her.

	3 Climax	
2 Rising Action		4 Falling Action
1 Beginning		5 Resolution/Ending

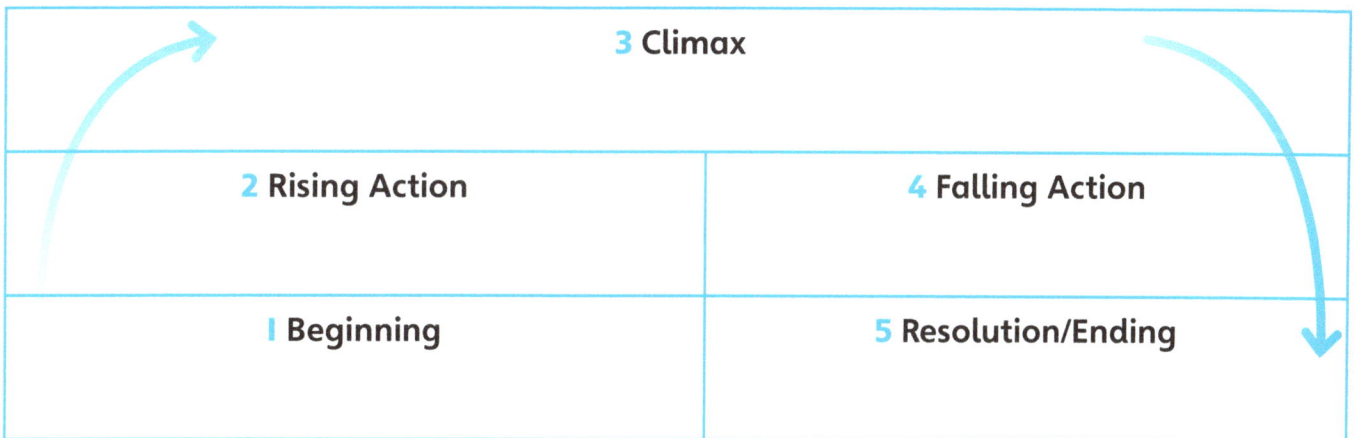

4 **Why do you think Amir sent the message in hieroglyphics? You can choose more than one answer. Mark ✓. Can you add your own idea?**

a He knew that Zahara loved everything about Egypt. ☐

b He knew she liked solving problems. ☐

c He wanted her to see that math is also about solving problems. ☐

d He thought she read hieroglyphics better than English. ☐

e My idea: _____

Grammar in Context

Reported Questions with *asked*

When we report a question, we usually use *ask*, change the pronouns, and use the past tense. We do not use question marks in reported questions. In reported questions with question words, we change the word order.

"What **are you going** to do, Amir?" Zahara asked.
         1   2   3

Zahara **asked** Amir what **he was going** to do.
                      2   1   3

With *yes/no* questions, we use *asked if*.

"**Do you understand the message?**" Zahara asked Amir.

Zahara **asked** Amir **if** he **understood** the message.

1 **Read and circle the correct answers.**

a "Do you like ice cream?" She asked me **if I liked** / **that I like** ice cream.

b "Can Petra speak Mandarin?" He asked him if **Petra could speak** / **can Petra speak** Mandarin.

c "What is Fabio doing?" Mike asked me **what is Fabio doing** / **what Fabio was doing**.

d "Where do your grandparents live?" She asked me where **my grandparents lived** / **did my grandparents live**.

2 **Write the words in the correct order.**

a color / I / your / was / asked / favorite / what / you

I _____.

b if / Janine / You / asked / animals / liked / she

You _____.

c when / My parents / vacation / me / summer / started / asked

My parents _____.

3 **Look at the picture and write the reported questions. Begin with *She asked me ... .***

a "Do you speak English?" _____

b "Where is your family from?" _____

c "What's your favorite myth?" _____

4 **Read the report. Write the police officer's four direct questions and the mystery man's three direct questions.**

Police Report

The mystery man arrived at 9 a.m. I asked him if he wanted to sit down. He had to wait for the detective who was investigating the murder. So I gave him a pen, and I asked him if he could fill out a form. After an hour, I asked him if he wanted something to eat, but he didn't. He asked me if he could have some more paper, and he continued writing. I asked him if he was thirsty. After three hours, he asked me if he could have another pen. Finally, he finished, and he asked me if I knew who the murderer was. I told him I just worked at the front desk.

The police officer's direct questions:

a Do you want to _____

b Can _____

c _____

d _____

The mystery man's direct questions:

e Can I have _____

f _____

g _____

My Life

Think of two interesting questions to ask people in your family. Write them here.

_____

_____

Ask your questions. Then, report the questions and answers here.

_____

_____

_____

Values: Respecting People from Other Cultures

1 Which of the following do you think are important parts of culture? Mark ✓.

	What I Think	What Michael Thinks		What I Think	What Michael Thinks
Traditions			Clothes		
Food			Meal Times		
Movies			Music		
Special Days			Books		
Cell phones			Sports		
Language			Your Ideas		

2 What does Michael think? Read what he says about culture. Mark ✓ the things that he talks about.

I think the most important parts of a culture are the traditions. In my class, there are students from lots of different cultures. That means they sometimes say, do, and eat different things because they are typical in each of their cultures. For example, David's mom is Irish, so he celebrates on March 17, which is an important day in Ireland. He brings in Irish flags to decorate the classroom and Irish food so that we can all celebrate together. Language is part of culture, too. So David calls his mom "mam." We made a poster with all the words the students in our class call their moms. There are ten different words, but they all mean "mom!" What do you do at your school to respect people from other cultures?

3 Find out about a different culture. Complete the fact sheet and draw a picture.

Country	
Languages Spoken	
An Important Festival in This Culture	
An Interesting Place to See	
A Famous Dish from This Culture	
Something Else That I Know About This Culture	

How Did I Do?

Check Your Oracy: Confident Use of Evidence to Support an Argument

1	I used evidence to support my argument.	**All the time / Most of the time / Sometimes**
2	I used the phrases on the cue cards.	**All of them / Most of them / Some of them**

The Big Challenge

How can we create our own language game?

a **What was the name of your game?**

_____

b **What type of game was it?**

_____

c **How well did you do? Color the stars to give yourself a score.***

I brainstormed ideas for a new language game and made a list.	☆☆☆☆☆
I created a new language game.	☆☆☆☆☆
I presented my game to the class.	☆☆☆☆☆
I listened carefully to my classmates' feedback about my game.	☆☆☆☆☆

*(5 = Awesome! 4 = Pretty good, 3 = OK, 2 = Could be better, 1 = Needs more work!)

d **Which other game did you like the best?**

_____

e **What could you do better next time?**

_____

The Big Question and Me

Because of the things I have learned in this unit,

I will _____

_____

SB pages 134–35

117

1 **Put the letters in the correct order and write the words.**

a m o j i e _____

b h s p a e _____

c g n i s _____

d m b l o s y _____

e e r i s g l p h i c o h y _____

2 **Choose the correct word to complete the sentences.**

> alphabet   bilingual   minority   multilingual   native speakers   population

Bragança is a district in northern Portugal, close to Spain. There is a ¹_____ language called Mirandese that is spoken by about 10% of the ²_____ of Bragança. Mirandese speakers are also ³_____ _____ of Portuguese, so they are ⁴_____.
Some people also speak Spanish, so they are ⁵_____. There is a written form of Mirandese, which, like Portuguese and Spanish, uses the Roman ⁶_____.

3 **Write the correct words to complete the sentences.**

a There are many ancient c _____ to learn about in history.

b There's a r _____ that we will have a new teacher next semester.

c This book is about the o _____ of names. My name is Felicity, and it means happy.

d L _____, all new stores and restaurants in the U.S.A. must be accessible for people with disabilities.

e What is the best way to c _____ with your friends?

f Some ideas are very a _____. They are sometimes difficult to understand.

4 What did Amir tell his mom about his conversation with Zahara?

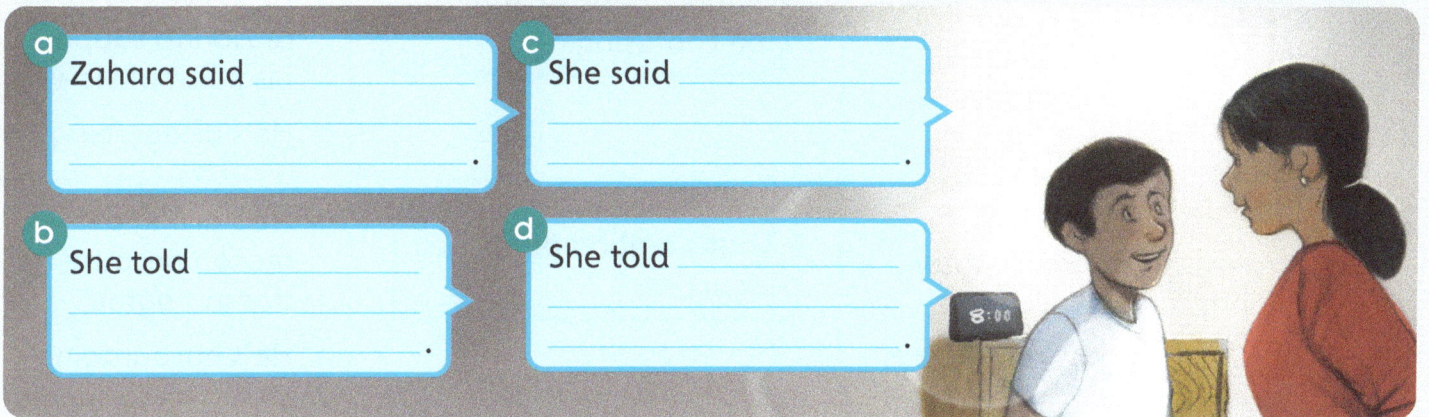

It is a text from my mom.

I am listening to music.

I am learning Spanish.

I want to buy a new video game.

a Zahara said _____ _____ _____ .

c She said _____ _____ _____ .

b She told _____ _____ _____ .

d She told _____ _____ _____ .

5 Your friends asked you lots of questions. Now, report them.

a "Do you have any brothers or sisters?"

He asked me _____ .

b "What's your favorite food?"

She asked me _____ .

c "Do we have any homework?"

She asked me _____ .

d "Can you play the piano?"

He asked me _____ .

6 Choose the correct connecting words to complete the paragraph.

in addition   however   therefore

My friend is French, so he speaks French. ¹_____, he speaks English.
²_____, I don't think he can write English very well. ³_____, he sends me emails to practice. It's fun!

Oracy Performance Task 2: Discussion

1 Answer the questions about the things your group chose.

a The most important phrase to know is _____.

b The thing we should never do is _____.

c The food we should definitely try is _____.

d The thing we should definitely see is _____.

2 What is the second speaker doing in each of these dialogues?

1 A visitor to our country has to know we have school on Saturdays.	I agree because it might be confusing.	a He's giving a reason to support his point of view. b He's disagreeing.
2 A visitor to our country has to know we have school on Saturdays.	That's a good point! Tell me more.	a He's giving a reason because he doesn't agree. b He's encouraging someone to speak.
3 A visitor to our country has to know we have school on Saturdays.	In my opinion, there are more important things to know.	a He's expressing his point of view. b He's encouraging someone to speak.

3 Put the words in the correct order.

a opinion / In / my _____

b disagree / I / because _____

c a / point / good / That's _____

d because / I / know /read / it / about _____

4 Write the phrase you like to use the most when you want to:

encourage someone to speak. _____

express your point of view. _____

disagree with evidence. _____

120

What can you remember about Unit 6? Do the quiz.

1 When was writing invented?

Around a 4500 BCE
b 500 BCE   c 45 BCE

2 How many languages disappear each year?

a 25   b 250   c 2500

3 What could Leanne legally do at the beginning of the story on page 126 in the Student's Book?

_____

4 Which of these is in *The Abandoned City* story?

a   b   c

5 Who did Leanne meet in *The Abandoned City*?

_____

6 What are these?

_____ .

7 People who can speak two languages are

_____

8 Report this statement.

She said she

_____

"I want to learn Italian."

9 Report this question.

I asked him _____

_____

"Why do you want to learn Spanish?"

10 How do you spell this?

_____

Check your answers in the Student's Book. How did you do?

8–10 ☐ Wow!   6–7 ☐ Good job!   0–5 ☐ Try harder!

? Why is language special? Write three things.

_____
_____
_____

7 How do machines help us?

1 ▶ 7.1 **Watch the video. Complete the graphic organizer.**

> move heavy objects   lever   travel from one place to another
> drone   crane   do our work   bike   pulley   solve problems
> communicate with each other   ramp   helicopter   robot

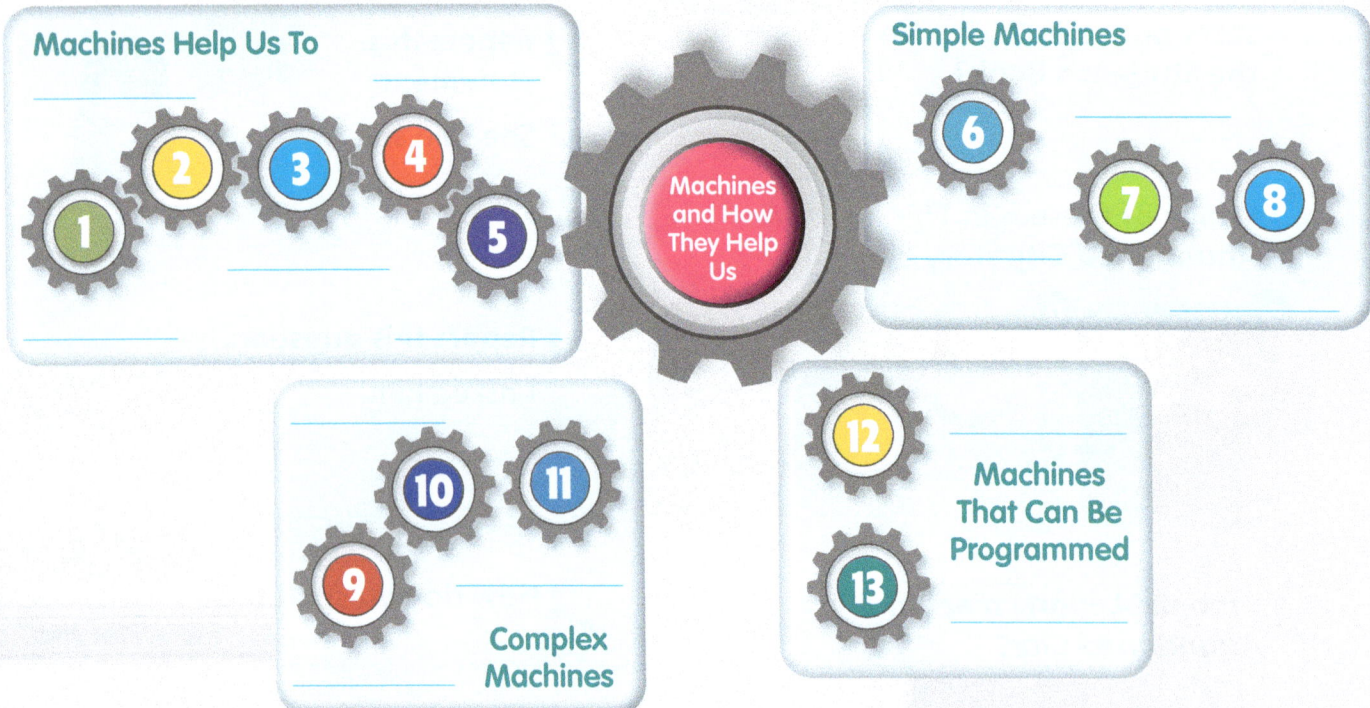

Machines Help Us To

_____ _____

1 2 3 4 5

Machines and How They Help Us

Simple Machines

6 7 8

Complex Machines

9 10 11

Machines That Can Be Programmed

12 13

2 Key Words 1 **Match the words with the pictures. Label the pictures S (simple machine) or C (complex machine).**

1 pulley
2 crane
3 lever
4 rollercoaster
5 Ferris wheel
6 ramp

 a
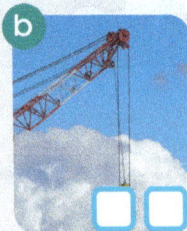 b
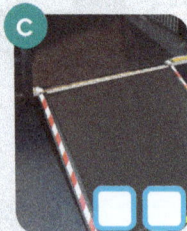 c
 d
 e
 f

1 Key Words 2 **Look at the picture. Complete the text with the correct words.**

accident   temperature   reached   chess

Mr. Ersoy and Mr. Kenter were playing ¹ _____ in a café when there was an
² _____ on the street in front of them. Mr. Kenter immediately called for an
ambulance, which ³ _____ the scene very quickly. No one was badly injured,
but one of the drivers said he was very hot. The ambulance driver took his
⁴ _____. It was very high, so they took him to the hospital. Then, Mr. Ersoy
and Mr. Kenter continued their chess game.

2 **Choose the correct words to complete the sentences.**

accurately   advancing   experience   repetitive   science-fiction   sensors

a I love _____ stories.

b Information technology is _____ all the time.

c It's important to use words _____.

d That story we read last month was too long and _____.

e Do you have any _____ of working with robots?

f There are different types of _____ that give us information about many
things, including temperature and light.

Reading Strategy: Main Idea and Supporting Details

The main idea is the most important idea in a text. Supporting details explain the main idea or give examples. Each section or paragraph of a text usually has its own main idea and supporting details.

1 **Read the text. Choose the best photograph to illustrate it. Mark ✓.**

Read of the Day | Gadgets & Tech | Games & Fun | More Cool Stuff

🛩 DRONES 🛩

We caught up with drone operator Louis McKennie in Silicon Valley, in California. He told us all about drones and what they can do.

CS: Can you tell us something about drones, Louis? Are they robots?

LMcK: That's a really good question because some people think that drones aren't robots. However, both robots and drones use complex computer software and can operate on their own. When many people hear the word "robot," they think of big machines that perform boring, repetitive tasks that people used to do. They also think robots have to look like humans, but they don't! Robots are everywhere, and drones are simply robots that can fly. Their scientific name is "Unmanned Aerial Vehicles" (UAVs), which means they are aircraft

that do not need pilots to fly. They use sensors and GPS (the Global Positioning System). Drones have many uses. They search for oil, help farmers check their crops, and find survivors after natural disasters. Perhaps your readers know that some pizza companies now use drones to make deliveries! And with Internet shopping becoming more popular, other companies are planning to use drones for their deliveries, too.

CS: I've heard about drones delivering pizzas, but a drone hasn't delivered one to me yet! Drones can also deliver more important things, can't they?

LMcK: Absolutely! In parts of Africa, drones deliver blood to doctors working a long way from big cities. In some places, delivering blood by car used to take many hours, but drones can reduce

that delivery time to just 45 minutes!

CS: How does it work?

LMcK: First, the doctor sends a text message to ask for blood. A drone is loaded with the blood, and it flies directly to its destination at speeds of up to 100 kph. A minute before the drone reaches its destination, the doctor gets a message. The drone then drops the blood, which has a parachute to help it land safely. And then it flies back to where it came from.

CS: What's the future of drones, do you think?

LMcK: I think they will be able to do a lot more in the future, but they won't be able to do some tasks for many years. But perhaps one day they'll be able to transport us to wherever we want to go—just like in science-fiction movies!

124

SB pages 140–43

Explore the Text

2 Read the text again. Circle the correct answers.

1 What is true about robots now, according to the text?

   a They can do jobs that no one wants to do.

   b They always look like humans.

   c They can take us wherever we want to go.

2 What is one of the key features of a drone?

   a It can fly accurately.

   b It doesn't have a pilot.

   c It looks for things.

3 What important job do drones now do in some parts of Africa?

   a They can quickly replace blood.

   b Hospitals no longer have to keep blood.

   c They deliver blood to doctors who are working a long way from big cities.

4 What do we learn about the time it takes drones to deliver blood?

   a It is about the same as before, when blood was delivered by car.

   b It takes longer than it used to.

   c It is much quicker than it used to be, when blood was delivered by car.

5 What happens to the drone after it has delivered the blood?

   a The doctor sends it back to the main hospital.

   b The drone returns on its own.

   c People collect the drones later in the day.

6 What does Louis think drones might be able to do in the future?

   a Deliver pizzas.

   b Take us anywhere.

   c Put us in science-fiction movies.

3 Complete the table with three supporting details for this main idea.

Main Idea: How Drones Deliver Blood in Africa		
Supporting Detail I	Supporting Detail 2	Supporting Detail 3
_____	_____	_____
_____	_____	_____

4 What do you think drones will be able to do in the future? Write your ideas.

I think drones will be able to fly to the moon.

I think drones will be able to collect trash.

I think drones will be able to _____ .

I think drones will be able to _____ .

Modal Verbs to Describe Future Ability

We use modal verbs of ability to talk about what we can or can't do. When we are talking about the future, we use *will/'ll be able to* and *will not/won't be able to* and a verb.

Perhaps drones will be able to transport us to wherever we want to go.
They won't be able to do some tasks for many years.

1 **Which sentences are about the future? Mark ✓.**

a People will be able to travel to Mars. ☐

b Robots are able to clean houses. ☐

c Robots won't be able to understand feelings. ☐

d People aren't able to remember as much as computers. ☐

2 **Write the words in the correct order.**

a able / my homework / to do / Robots / will / be

_____

b to eat / be / able / food / won't / Robots

_____

c take / to / my temperature / Robots / be / will / able

_____

d won't / be / to laugh / Robots / able

_____

e able / our grocery shopping / to / will / be / Robots / do

_____

3 **Look at the pictures. Complete the sentences using *will be able to* or *won't be able to*.**

a Robots _____ ride horses.

b Robots _____ pick up trash.

c Robots _____ drink juice in a café.

d Trains _____ fly in the sky.

Speak to me!

e Animals _____ speak English.

f We _____ smell through computers.

That smells so good!

4 **Read and complete the letter with *will* or *won't be able to* and the verbs in parentheses.**

March 24, 2120

Dear Parents,

Next year, Class 6A [1]_____ (visit) the school star, Planet XYZ. However, younger brothers and sisters [2]_____ (go) on this trip because they are too young. Also, please note that parents [3]_____ (come along) because there isn't enough room in the school rocket this year.

On the trip, children [4]_____ (attend) all classes as usual. However, they [5]_____ (play) regular sports.

Parents [6]_____ (speak) to their children through the school space portal each evening.

For more information, please go to the school star website.

Sincerely

Charlotte Dwyer

Principal

5 **Complete the sentences. Use two of the three verbs given.**

a   change / have / repair

1   Sophia ___won't be able to change___ her bicycle tire herself because she is too young.

2   Her cousin Pedro _____ it because he knows a lot about bikes.

b   come / reply / help

1   Fiona _____ to your house today because she is sick at the moment.

2   She is sorry, but she _____ you with your homework.

My Life

Complete the sentences with your ideas.

In the future, I think people _____.

When I'm 16, _____.

By this time next year, I _____.

Spelling Patterns and Word Study

1 Look at the pictures and write the words. They all have the same sound.

germs   heard   shirt   nurse   words

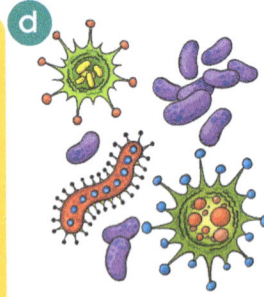

a

b

c

d

e

2 Match the pictures with the correct spellings of the word pictured.

1

2

3

4

5

a ir

b ur

c or

d er

e ear

Oracy

1 In Oracy Time! you talked about your robot. Write the three best things it can do.

_____

_____

_____

2 Which phrase(s) did you use to check that everyone could hear you?

_____

3 Did you use these phrases when other people were presenting? Mark ✓.

Can you speak more slowly? ☐   Can you speak up? ☐

7A

It's and its

It's = It is or It has.

It's cute! = It is cute.

It's swum in the ocean. = It has swum in the ocean.

Remember its is the possessive form of the pronoun it. There is no apostrophe.

The animal has a big head, but its body isn't very long.

A cute robotic dog for a pet?

1 **Circle the correct words to complete the sentences.**

a Look at that cute robotic dog! **It's / Its** playing a game with **it's / its** owner!

b Put the book back in **it's / its** place.

c I can't see the hummingbird any more. I think **it's / its** flown away.

d **It's / Its** time for bed.

e Our city is famous for **it's / its** beautiful old buildings.

f Many people think **it's / its** nice to have a cat.

2 **Complete the sentences with it's or its. Where you write it's, is it short for it has or it is? Write the full form after each sentence.**

a _____It's_____ my pen, not yours! _____It is_____

b The school is flooded, and it has canceled all _____ classes today.

_____

c Look at this book! _____ pages are different colors! _____

d _____ been a long time since I saw my piano teacher. _____

e _____ difficult to do this exercise. _____

f _____ been raining all day! _____

1 READ Look at the report on page 147 in the Student's Book. Answer the questions.

a What is the topic of Sam's report? _____

b Did he enjoy it? What word tells you? _____

c Why can his favorite invention reach difficult places? _____

d What does it have on its head? _____

e What other use does Sam suggest for it? _____

2 PLAN You are going to write a report about a show or market you have been to recently. Write the name of the show or market in the middle of the graphic organizer, and then make notes.

LOCATION _____   **DATE**
_____   _____

DESCRIPTION _____   **MY FAVORITE PART**
_____   **AND WHY I LIKED IT**
_____   _____
_____   _____
_____   _____
_____   _____
_____   _____

3 WRITE Use your notes to write your report.

4 EDIT Read your work and mark ✓.

Did you:

● include the date, the place, and a description? ☐

● say what you liked the best and why? ☐

● use *its* and *it's* correctly? ☐

Ready to Read: Fiction

1 **Key Words 4** **Look at Jackie's photo. Label the things.**

> coconut palms   hut   matches   oil drums   paper   plastic sheet
> raft   sail   sticks   stones   tires   vines

a v_____

b h_____

c p_____

d c_____

e s_____

f t_____

g s_____

h m_____

i o_____

j s_____

k p_____

l r_____

2 **Complete Jackie's sentences with the correct words from Activity I.**

a Lots of _____ and _____ grow on our tropical island.

b Our oil is stored in _____ .

c Yesterday we made a fire with _____ and _____ and
lit it with _____ .

d We put _____ around the fire.

e The _____ stops our things from getting wet in the rain.

f When we arrived, the _____ only had an old table inside it.

g I made a _____ with some old car _____ .

h The _____ is made from very strong material.

Reading Strategy: Making Connections

When you read, try to link what you are reading about to your own experience. It might be something that has happened to you, something you read in a book or saw in a movie, or perhaps something that happened to other people.

1 Read the story. What are the two names of the knot the children learn?

a _____ or _____ knot

CHAPTER 5
Maeve, Robert, and Sam Go to Camp

"Hi, I'm Julie, head camp counselor," said the smiling woman as she welcomed Maeve, Robert, and Sam.

It was Friday evening, and the three children were going to spend the weekend camping outdoors.

"Come and meet the other children," Julie continued. "Dinner's ready!"

Maeve, Robert, and Sam sat down to eat around the campfire with nine other children, all looking excited and happy.

"Welcome again, everyone," Julie said as they were eating. "OK. The highlight of the weekend is the raft race across the river on Sunday."

"WOW!" Maeve exclaimed. "Are we going to build the rafts?"

"Yes, we are!" Julie replied.

The next morning, the children gathered around Julie on the riverbank.

"How are we going to build the rafts, Julie?" Sam asked. "I've never done anything like this before."

"First, you need to learn how to tie special knots. Do any of you know how to tie a reef knot?"

"Are reef knots the same as square knots?"

Robert asked. "If they are, then I can tie them."

"And I can, too," said Maeve.

How to Tie a Reef Knot

"Great," Julie said. "You can help teach the others. Give everyone a piece of blue and a piece of red string, Robert. Maeve, can you show us how to tie a reef knot?"

"Take your two pieces of string," Maeve began. "First, cross the red piece over the blue piece and under, and then cross them again, the blue over the red and under this time. Pull the ends tight, and you have your reef knot."

"Thanks, Maeve," Julie said. "Now, let's all practice tying reef knots."

"You could put us into two groups, Julie," Sam suggested. "Robert can work with one group, and Maeve with the other."

"That's a great idea," said Julie. Soon they could all tie reef knots.

"Great," Julie said. "Let's start building the rafts! Here are some plastic sheets, some wood, and some old car tires. Don't forget to make a sail for your raft. I would plan the rafts very carefully. I wouldn't build them too fast."

Both groups worked hard for the rest of the day. They tied branches together with reef knots. Maeve's group made a sail from a plastic sheet, and Robert's group put some old tires under the branches of their raft to make it float better. Then, the children tried out their rafts on the river before dinner.

"Today has been awesome!" Sam said.

"I wonder which raft will win the race across the river tomorrow," Julie said.

SB pages 149–54

2 **Read the story again. Put the sentences in the correct order.**

a Sam asked how they were going to build the rafts. ☐

b Julie took Maeve, Robert, and Sam to eat dinner around the campfire. ☐

c Both groups tested their rafts on the water. ☐

d The children practiced tying reef, or square, knots. ☐

e Julie, the head camp counselor, welcomed Maeve, Robert, and Sam. ☐

f Julie said the highlight of the weekend was the raft race on Sunday. ☐

3 **Read the story again. Who said ... ?**

a "Welcome again, everyone!" _____

b "I've never done anything like this before." _____

c "Are reef knots the same as square knots?" _____

d "Can you show us how to tie a reef knot?" _____

e "Pull the ends tight." _____

f "Today has been awesome!" _____

g "You could put us into two groups." _____

4 **Look at these knots. Which ones can you tie? Mark ✓.**

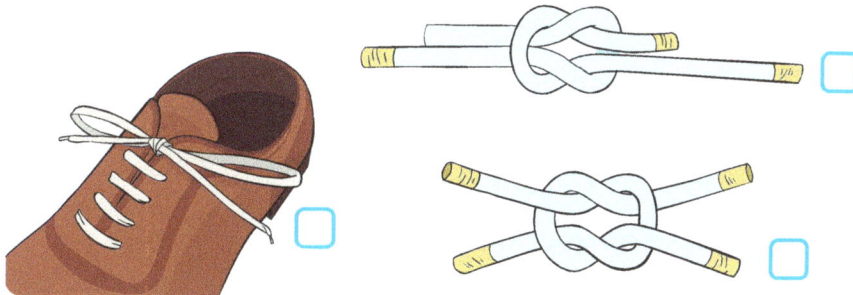

5 **Have you ever gone to camp? If so, where did you go? What was the best thing about it? If not, would you like to go? Why?**

_____
_____
_____
_____
_____
_____

Grammar in Context

Could and would for Ideas and Advice

We use *You could* to suggest possible solutions to a problem.
You could put us into two groups.
We use *I would* or *I wouldn't* to make a stronger suggestion and give advice.
I would plan the rafts very carefully. **I wouldn't** build them too fast.

1 **Complete the sentences giving advice.**
Then, match the advice with the problems.

1 You _____ read
your book.

2 I _____ look at
a screen after 9 p.m.

3 I _____ order
a pizza.

4 You _____ go
to bed earlier.

a I'm always tired.

b Right now, I'm really hungry.

Healthy dial-a-pizza (025-768)

c I'm so bored.

d I can't get to sleep.

1:00

2 **Circle the correct word to complete Ben's advice to you.**

a You   It's raining. The matches are getting wet.

Ben   I **could** / **would** / **wouldn't** put them in the hut.

b You   The raft needs a sail.

Ben   You **could** / **would** / **wouldn't** use a plastic sheet.

c You   I can't open this coconut! I'm really thirsty.

Ben   I **would** / **could** / **wouldn't** use a stone to open it!

d You   There's a large black spider on your book.

Ben   Urgh! How horrible! I **would** / **wouldn't** / **could** touch it.

e You   I'm hungry. Can I eat these berries?

Ben   I **could** / **would** / **wouldn't** eat them because they are poisonous.

3 **Complete the sentences with *could*, *would*, or *wouldn't*.**

a I _____ buy that coat. It's too big for you.

b I _____ call your mom. She's probably worrying about you.

c You _____ do your homework after dinner if you don't have time now.

d I _____ study hard for your test. It's going to be difficult!

4 Read the letters. Complete Aunt Esmeralda's reply with *would*, *could*, or *wouldn't*.

Dear Aunt Esmeralda,

I want to ride my bike to the drugstore in town to buy candy and ice cream on Saturdays, but my mom and dad won't let me. They say I'm too young—but I'm 12, and all my friends meet at the store on Saturdays. It's not fair. I don't want to do anything bad. I just want to hang out with my friends and eat some candy and ice cream!

Please give me some advice.

Melanie

Dear Melanie,

First of all, put yourself in your parents' place. I ¹_____ think about why they won't let you go to the drugstore with your friends. Perhaps they worry when you're away from the house for a long time. I ²_____ suggest that you make a plan, and then you ³_____ talk about it with your parents. I ⁴_____ go out for very long the first few times. Then, your parents will see that you are sensible. Do you think your parents are worried about the candy and ice cream? If so, perhaps you ⁵_____ say you'll only eat a little ice cream. I ⁶_____ say anything about candy because everyone knows it's bad for you! Good luck!

Aunt Esmeralda

5 Look at the picture of Billie and his brother Ryan. Billie wants to play soccer after school. Complete Ryan's suggestions.

Billie Who will pick me up?

Ryan I _____ ask mom or get a ride with a friend.

Billie I can't play soccer very well.

Ryan I _____ worry. You'll learn soon.

Billie My shoes are too small.

Ryan You _____ ask mom to buy you some new ones.

Billie I don't know where my friends are playing today.

Ryan I _____ ask someone.

My Life

What would you say to your friend in these situations? Use *You could*, *I would*, or *I wouldn't*.

Your friend I share my bedroom with my little sister. It's hard to study because she is always so noisy.

You _____

Your friend I want to get on to the soccer team.

You _____

Values: Being Resourceful

1 **Think back to the story *A Lost Journal* on page 150 in the Student's Book. Answer the questions.**

   a What problem(s) did the writer have at the beginning of his time on the island?

   b Why did he make a lever from a branch and vines?

   c What problem did the writer solve by eating beetles?

2 **Was the writer resourceful? Look at the infographic. Did he follow the three steps?**

3 **In which of these situations is it important to be resourceful? Mark ✓.**

   a when you do your homework ☐

   b when you are watching a movie ☐

   c when you have a problem ☐

4 **Look at this list of situations. Choose one and decide how you can be resourceful. Make notes on the paper.**

   a You have to make dinner for your family, but have no gas or electricity. You do have $15.

   b You have to think of three different ways to use a yogurt container.

   c You are lost in a foreign city, you don't speak the language, and you don't have your phone.

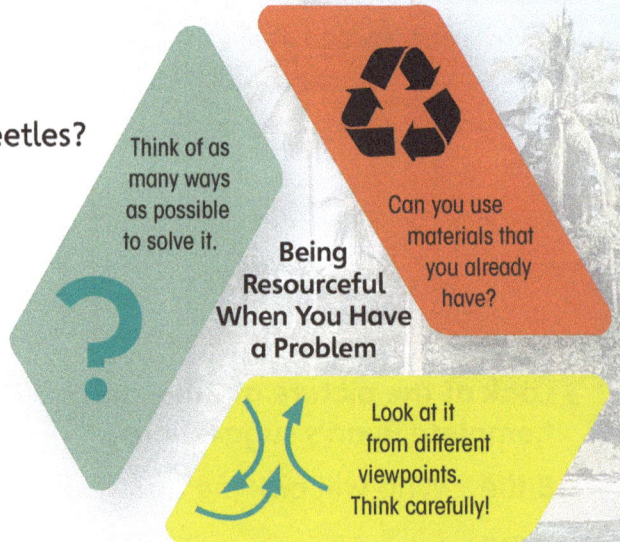

Think of as many ways as possible to solve it.

Being Resourceful When You Have a Problem

Can you use materials that you already have?

Look at it from different viewpoints. Think carefully!

Check Your Oracy: Projecting Your Voice

1	I tried to project my voice.	**All the time / Most of the time / Sometimes**
2	I asked if people could hear me.	**At the beginning / During my presentation**
3	I used the phrases on the cue cards.	**All of them / Most of them / Some of them**

The Big Challenge   STEAM: Technology & Engineering

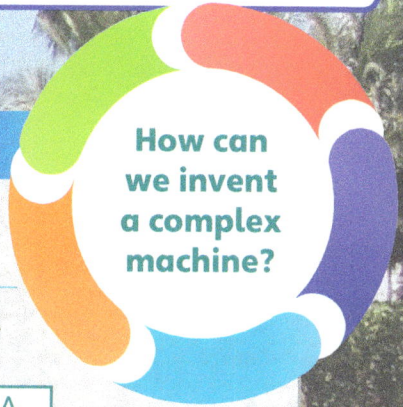

How can we invent a complex machine?

a **What jobs did you want a machine to do for you?**

_____

b **How well did you do? Color the stars to give yourself a score.***

I thought of ideas for my machine.	☆☆☆☆☆
I drew a design for my machine.	☆☆☆☆☆
I gave my presentation to the class.	☆☆☆☆☆
I projected my voice during my presentation.	☆☆☆☆☆

*(5 = Awesome! 4 = Pretty good, 3 = OK, 2 = Could be better, I = Needs more work!)

c **Which other idea did you like the best?**

_____

d **What could you do better next time?**

_____

The Big Question and   Me

In this unit, I learned how machines help us.

I learned that _____.

I learned that _____.

1 Look at the picture and label the things.

crane Ferris wheel drone rollercoaster ramp

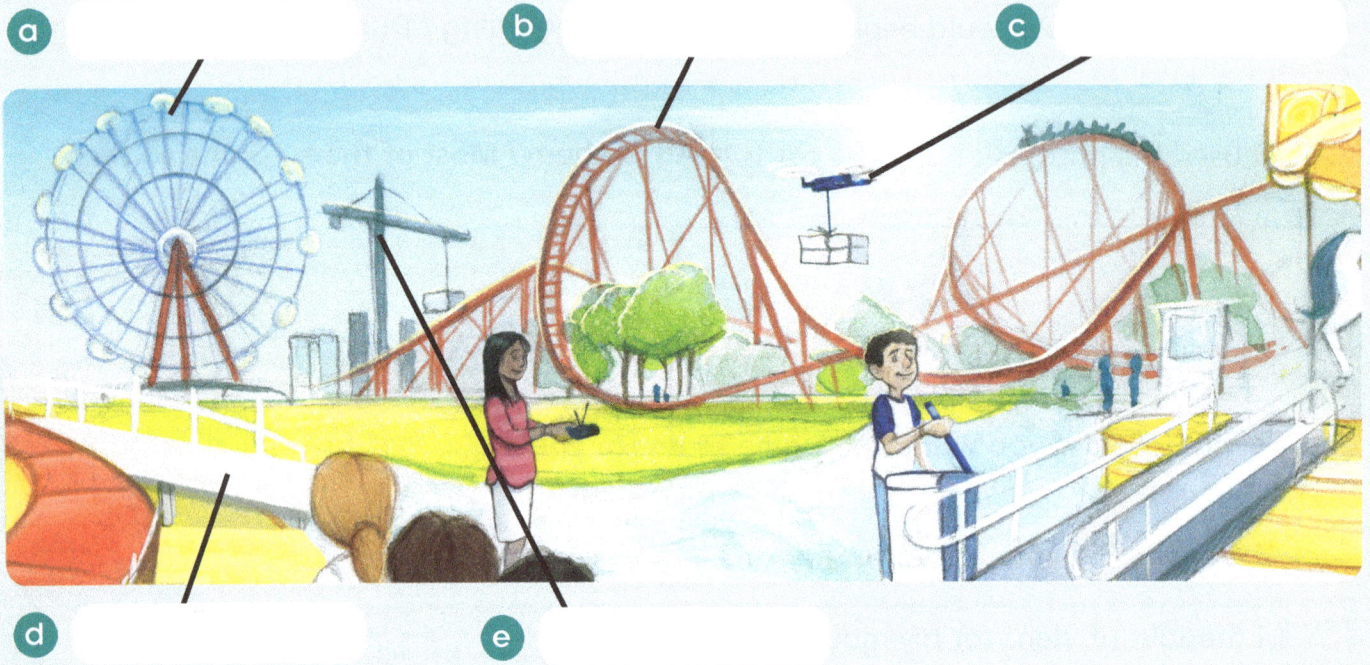

a _____

b _____

c _____

d _____

e _____

2 Choose the correct words to complete the sentences.

sticks sensors simple sails stone science

a _____ machines help us to move things.

b My sister enjoys watching _____ -fiction movies. I prefer drama.

c Many cars have _____ that make them easy to park.

d Some boats have very big _____.

e If you want to make a fire, you need some _____.

f Some houses are made of _____.

3 Look at the pictures. What can you see through the key holes? Write the words.

a b c d e f

c_____t   t__e   m_____s   h_t   v__e   p_____y

4 Complete the sentences with *will be able to* or *won't be able to*.

> The future! In 20 years' time …

a Robots _____ wash the dishes.　　b People _____ fly.

c Cars _____ park in cities.　　d Robots _____ clean up our oceans.

5 Your friend has to do some homework about a machine. You have some ideas and advice. Complete the sentences with *could*, *would*, or *wouldn't*.

a I _____ find out about the factory where they make the devices.

b You _____ ask the receptionist at the office for help.

c I _____ trust all the information you find on the Internet. It isn't always correct.

d You _____ ask your friends if they have any information.

e I _____ use too many pictures. The teacher wants us to write a lot.

6 Complete the text with *it's* or *its*. Circle the one that means *it has*.

★★★★★

"What a machine! The new driverless car is amazing! [1]_____ not for everyone. But if you have physical disabilities, or if you just don't enjoy driving, [2]_____ the car for you. [3]_____ sensors turn on the lights if [4]_____ dark, and [5]_____ parking skills are superb! The car does [6]_____ work, and you can do yours! [7]_____ changed my life!"

Li Lang, driverless car owner

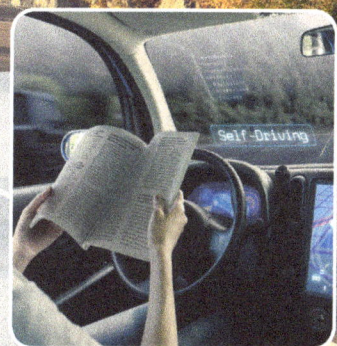

SPEAKING MISSION

1 **Put the letters in the correct order and write the words.**

a aptebrol idaem lyarpe

_ _ _ _ _ _ _ _ _ _

_ _ _ _ _ _

_ _ _ _ _ _

b mage conlsoe _ _ _ _ _ _

_ _ _ _ _ _

c rgecahre _ _ _ _ _ _ _ _

d tnrarawy _ _ _ _ _ _ _ _

e eprrai _ _ _ _ _ _

f ecnres _ _ _ _ _ _

g myemor _ _ _ _ _ _

h ecdiev _ _ _ _ _ _

2 **Complete the sentences with the correct words from Activity I.**

a I usually _____ my cell phone battery overnight.

b When you buy something new, it's important to keep the _____ .

c My favorite _____ is my cell phone.

d We have a _____ for long car trips to watch movies, play games, and listen to music.

e My phone doesn't work, so I'm going to get someone to _____ it.

f My friend has broken the _____ on her cell phone!

g The _____ is full. I can't save these photos.

h I love playing on my _____ .

3 **What does Lisa say to Joey? Put the dialogue in the correct order.**

Joey Hello. How can I help you?

Lisa 1 _e_

Joey What's wrong?

Lisa 2 ____

Joey Oh, no. Did you drop it?

Lisa 3 ____

Joey When did you buy it?

Lisa 4 ____

Joey OK, I can fix it for you, but it isn't under warranty.

Lisa 5 ____

Joey It should be ready in about 30 minutes. It will cost $150.

a Hmmm. Yes, I did.

b Two years ago, I think.

c The screen is broken.

d OK, thank you. How long will it take?

e Hello. I have a problem with my cell phone.

140

What can you remember about Unit 7? Do the quiz.

1 Who made drawings of a robotic man over 500 years ago?

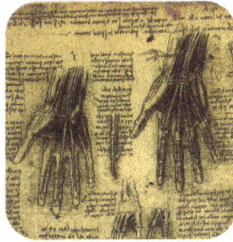

_____

2 What very difficult game can robots beat us at?

_____

3 Where does a robot store information?

In its _____

4 Where was the author of *A Lost Journal* sailing to?

a Papua New Guinea
b The Solomon islands   c Fiji

5 Which food did the author of *A Lost Journal* not eat?

a fish   b beetles   c crab

6 What is this?

It's a _____ .

7 Which of these things can you use to tie branches together?

a coconuts   b vines   c sticks

8 Complete the sentence.

We _____
_____ go on vacation to the moon in the near future.

9 Your friends haven't finished their homework. What do you say?

You _____ ask your teacher to give you more time.

10 What was the oracy skill for this unit?

_____

Check your answers in the Student's Book. How did you do?

8–10 ☐ Wow!   6–7 ☐ Good job!   0–5 ☐ Try harder!

?  **How do machines help us?** Write three things.

_____
_____
_____

8 How do we know what happened in the past?

1 ▶ 8.1 **Watch the video. Complete the graphic organizer.**

> workplaces   documents   houses   art   jewelry   the Valley of the Kings
> gold death mask   theaters   tombs   manuscripts   tools

Archeological Sites

1 _____
2 _____
3 _____
4 _____
5 _____

The Past Is All Around Us

Artifacts

6 _____
7 _____
8 _____
9 _____
10 _____
11 _____

2 **Key Words 1** **Match the words with the definitions.**

1	monument	a	a person who writes about or studies the past
2	historian	b	a valuable yellow metal
3	discovery	c	a book, musical composition, or document written by hand
4	tomb	d	bones and teeth are examples
5	document	e	a building or structure that is built to make people remember an event in history or a famous person
6	manuscript	f	a piece of paper with official written information on it
7	remains	g	when someone finds something for the first time
8	gold	h	a place where a dead person is buried

1 **Key Words 2** **Choose the correct words to complete the sentences.**

> Bronze Age   carbon   century   date   decay   legend

a Some people think that the Beaker People brought bronze to Britain during the _____ .

b When archeologists _____ objects, they find out how old they are.

c They can measure the amount of a type of _____ in the remains of humans, animals, and plants to see how old they are.

d Weather makes objects _____ over time.

e My grandmother was born in the 20th _____ .

f One of my favorite stories is a medieval _____ about a king and a princess.

2 **Look at the pictures. Write the words.**

> detective   horn   pottery   thumb

a

b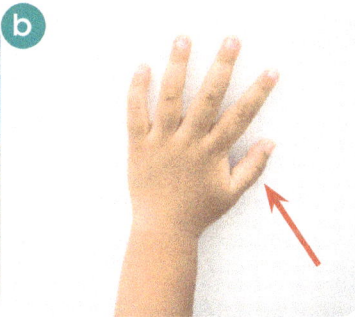

c

d

3 **Answer the questions.**

a How long is your thumb?

_____

b Which century are we living in?

_____

c What can cause teeth to decay?

_____

d Can you name two fictional detectives?

_____ and _____

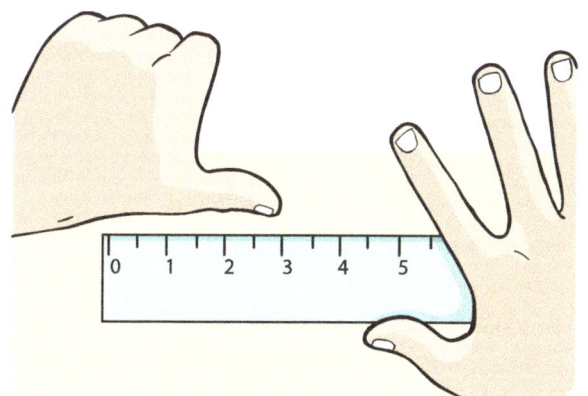

1 Read Jordie's text message. Look at the underlined words. Which photo did she send? Mark ✓.

a

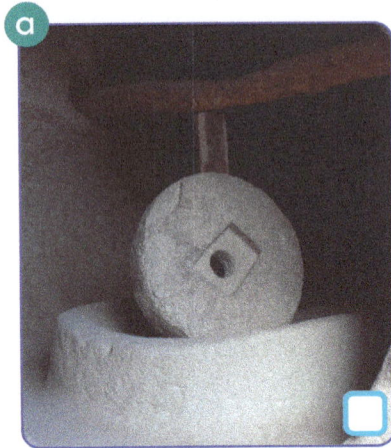

Hey! At the museum with school. Cool! These are <u>grinding stones</u>. Awesome! Two stones—a lower stone and an upper stone. The <u>lower stone</u> is long! I think I could hold the <u>upper stone</u> in my hand, but the <u>lower stone</u> looks very heavy. What do you think they're for?

b

2 Read Jordie's report. What were the stones used for? _____

OUR FIELD TRIP

Last week, our class went on a field trip to the local museum. There's an interesting exhibition on at the moment about the Bronze Age. We started studying objects, or artifacts, from that time last semester. Our teacher, Mr. Martinez, thought this exhibition would be perfect for us, and it was!

Before we went, Mr. Martinez put the class into groups. Each group had to think of a question to find the answer to in the museum. "You're going to be history detectives!" he said.

I was in a group with Thomas, Edward, and Emily. We all love food, so we wanted to know what Bronze Age people ate. Edward thought they probably ate vegetables, but we weren't sure. So our question was: What did Bronze Age people eat?

When we arrived at the museum, the director, Mrs. Williams, took us on a tour of the Bronze Age exhibition. It was fascinating. She explained that the artifacts in the exhibition were over 3,000 years old. The archeologists and historians who put together the exhibition had to be very careful because the objects are primary sources—they were used by real Bronze Age people!

After the tour, we had an hour to explore by ourselves and find the answer to our group's question. We looked at two parts of the exhibition in particular: farming and life at home. We learned that wheat, barley, and other grains were grown by farmers. Then, the "heads" of grain were dried in pots near fires in the houses. After that, they were ground into flour on grinding stones. There were some grinding stones in the exhibition. The flour was used to make bread, and yeast was added to make the bread rise.

There was a model of the inside of a Bronze Age house in the exhibition, and we could see pottery and cups made of horn. We also saw loaves of bread, vegetables, and fruit. We had the answer to our question! Before we left, we checked it with Mrs. Williams. She explained that people in the Bronze Age also ate meat, but not very often.

By Jordie Allen

Explore the Text

Reading Strategy: Monitor and Clarify

It's important to check that you understand what you have just read. You can do this by monitoring—thinking about what you do and don't understand—and by clarifying— finding out or checking.

3 Jordie's friend Kevin, who did not go on the school trip, has just read her report. He didn't understand everything. He had to monitor and clarify. Complete his table.

Monitor and Clarify		
I didn't understand:	I used these strategies:	Now I think it means: 😊
explore	I looked for clues in the text.	It means looking around to see new and interesting things.
a **Yeast** was added to make the bread rise.	I asked myself questions about bread. I read the text again slowly.	Yeast _____
b _____	I looked for clues in the text.	It's the past participle of *grind*.

4 Match the questions with the answers.

1 Which historical period is Jordie learning about in school?

2 What happened at the beginning of the visit to the museum?

3 What were the primary sources?

4 How old were the primary sources?

5 What was the answer to Jordie's group's question?

a The students were shown around the exhibition by the director.

b the Bronze Age artifacts

c Bronze Age people mainly ate bread, vegetables, and fruit. They sometimes ate meat.

d the Bronze Age

e over 3,000 years old

5 Read the information about a new exhibition. Imagine you are going to the exhibition. What would your question be?

_____

_____

New Exhibition
Pottery from the Bronze Age

Come and find out about pottery from 3,000 years ago!
Open Tues.–Sun. 9 a.m.–5 p.m.
CLOSED ON MONDAYS.

FREE ADMISSION

The Past Simple Passive Voice

We use the past simple passive voice for actions in the past when we don't know who did the action or it isn't important who did the action. We form the past simple passive with *was/were* + past participle. If we want to say who did the action, we use *by*.

Yeast **was added** to make the bread rise.

Wheat, barley, and other grains **were grown by** farmers.

1 **Read the sentences and complete with *was* or *were*.**

a The grinding stones _____ used to make flour.

b Water and yeast _____ added to the mixture.

c The bread _____ cooked on an open fire.

d The artifact _____ exhibited in a museum.

2 **Put the words in the correct order to make sentences.**

a at school / The photographs / were / shown

_____

b ancient stone / found / An / on / farm / the / was

_____

c all parents / to / sent / was / An email

_____

d were / All flights / bad weather / because of / canceled

_____

3 **Rewrite these sentences using the past simple passive.**

a People decorated documents.

Documents were decorated.

b In prehistoric times, people ate bread.

_____

c The author wrote the book in Spanish.

_____

d Archeologists made important discoveries.

_____

146

4 **Complete the text. Use the past simple passive of the verbs in parentheses.**

How Were Books Made in the Past?

The first people to make books were the Ancient Egyptians. Papyrus "paper" ¹_____ (make) from the stems of the papyrus plant. Then, individual sheets of paper ²_____ (glue) together to make scrolls. In India, palm leaves ³_____ (put) together, and then pieces of wood ⁴_____ (place) on either side of them. These methods took a long time because all the work ⁵_____ (do) by hand.

In the 15th century, the printing press ⁶_____ (invent) in Germany, and after that, books ⁷_____ (produce) more quickly.

5 **Write sentences about the pictures using the past simple passive. Use the information to help you.**

a

b

c

The Gateway Arch / open / in 1967

These pieces of pottery / find / in Greece

A rocket / launch / into space

a _____

b _____

c _____

My Life

Find out about a historical object in your house, school, or city. Draw and write about it.

This is a writing box. It was made in Victorian times in England. It was used by people who wrote lots of letters. Pens and ink were stored in it. Also, a photo was kept in this writing box.

_____
_____
_____
_____

1 Label the pictures. Circle the words where *gh* makes the sound *f*.

high   cough   bright   rough

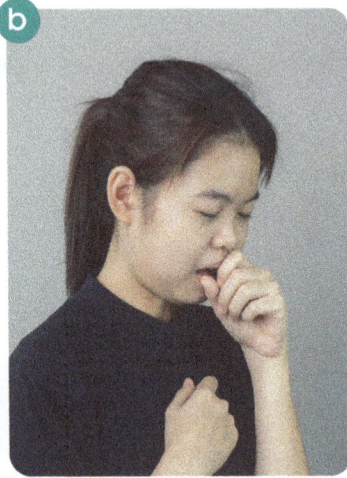

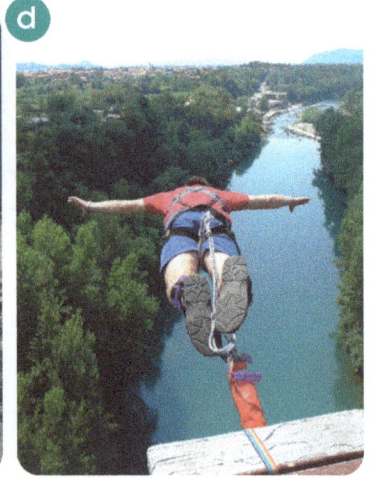

a

b

c

d

2 Circle the words where the *gh* is silent.

eight   light   laugh   thought   enough   taught   tough   dough

Oracy

1 Which Oracy Time! topic did you choose for your story?
Mark ✓.

⭐ **Oracy Time!**

Think of a time when you:
- found something interesting. ☐
- went to an interesting place for the first time. ☐
- tried something new. ☐

And I found this!

2 What sentence did you use to begin your story?

3 Did you look at your audience and use appropriate body movements when you were telling your story?

Non-defining Relative Clauses

We use non-defining relative clauses when we want to add extra information to a sentence. We use commas to show that the information is extra.
My friend Lisa, who lives in Australia, **is 12 years old.**
I visited the KidsHistory website, which Lisa told me about.
who = people, *which* = things, places
We cannot use *that* in a non-defining relative clause.

1 **Read the pairs of sentences. Then, combine them to make one sentence with a non-defining relative clause.**

a Howard Carter discovered the tomb of Tutankhamun. He was born in 1874.
Howard Carter, who discovered the tomb of Tutankhamun, was born in 1874.

b These grinding stones were used to make flour. They are thousands of years old.

_____

c I went to my cousin Susannah's party. I really liked it.

_____

d My Uncle Stuart is a vet. He lives in London.

_____

e Madrid is the capital of Spain. It's one of my favorite cities.

_____

f The Pyramids of Teotihuacán are in Mexico. They were built around 100 BCE.

_____

2 **Complete the sentences with *who* or *which*.**

a Jake's grandparents, _____who_____ are on vacation, called him last night.

b Mexico City, _____ has a population of nearly 9 million, is one of the largest cities in the world.

c My neighbor Jean Claude, _____ lives on a farm, is a really nice person.

d My cousin Sam, _____ lives in Hong Kong, has just been accepted to City College.

e Amsterdam, _____ has many canals, was a very important city in 17th-century Europe.

f The White House, _____ has 132 rooms, is the official residence of the president of the U.S.A.

Writing

1 **READ** Look at the biography on page 169 in the Student's Book. Answer the questions.

a How many different jobs did Leonardo have? What were they?

_____

b Do we know who the woman in the *Mona Lisa* was?

_____

c What does the author think is more interesting: Leonardo's paintings or his inventions?

_____

2 **PLAN** You are going to write a biography about a famous person. Make notes in the graphic organizer.

An introduction to the person:

An interesting detail about their life:

Who?

Key dates in the person's life:

Your opinion about the person:

3 **WRITE** Use your notes to write your biography.

4 **EDIT** Read your work and mark ✓.

Did you:

● introduce the person? ☐

● include key dates and interesting details? ☐

● express your opinion? ☐

● use non-defining relative clauses? ☐

Ready to Read: Fiction

1 | Key Words 4 | **Choose the correct words to label the picture.**

> fountain   villa   aqueduct   cobblestones   column   tiles   fresco

a _____

d _____

c _____

e _____

g _____

f _____

b _____

2 **Choose the correct words to complete the paragraph.**

> foundations   grid   roads   straight

As well as beautiful villas, aqueducts, and theaters, the Romans built excellent
¹_____ . Many of them are still used today. Like Roman buildings,
these roads had strong ²_____ . They were very ³_____ ,
and, in the towns and cities, they were built on a ⁴_____ pattern.

1 **Read the story. What does Hunter want to be when he's grown up?** _____

A Place Called Mérida

"How was school?" asked Hunter's mom. She asked him the same question every evening. He hated answering her because he didn't like school much. The only class he really liked to talk about was history. He loved history.

"We had a great history class today," he said. "We learned about the Roman Empire."

"That's good," said his mom, who didn't share his love of history. "By the way, I have a video call later with Auntie Rita."

Auntie Rita was his mom's best friend. She lived in Spain with her husband, who was an archeologist, and their three cats. After dinner, Hunter went to his room to do his science homework. He was putting on his headphones when he heard his mom talking in the kitchen.

"So it's nearly 40°C, but your visitors want to explore Mérida! They must be crazy!"

When Hunter heard the name Mérida, he started to listen carefully. His history teacher had talked about a place in Spain called Mérida in class that morning. "It must be the same place," he thought. He knew that there were two Méridas—one in Europe and one in Mexico. "It can't be the Mérida in Mexico because Auntie Rita lives in Spain."

He opened his history book and started to read the part about Mérida..

> Mérida was founded in 25 BCE by the Emperor Augustus for Roman soldiers who were at the end of their career in the army. In those days, it was called Emerita Augusta.

Then, Hunter heard Auntie Rita's voice. "And now they want to close the Roman bridge …"

Hunter ran into the kitchen.

"Sorry to interrupt, Mom, but do you live in Mérida, Auntie Rita—Mérida with the amazing Roman aqueduct?"

"Yes, I do! Why?"

Hunter spent the next hour asking Auntie Rita questions about Mérida. She showed him a piece of pottery that her husband had found on an archeological site in the city.

"He brought it home to clean," she explained. "What do you think it is?"

Hunter looked at the screen. "It might be made of stone, but I think it's pottery. It's a beautiful pitcher. It was probably for water."

"You're right, Hunter!" said Auntie Rita.

"That's awesome!" said Hunter, who was having the best history lesson ever.

His mom looked at him proudly. "Wow! I had no idea you knew so much history!"

Hunter smiled. "You know I want to be an archeologist when I grow up, Mom."

2 **Read the text again. Circle the correct answers.**

1 How did Hunter feel when his mom asked him about his day at school?

a happy   b angry   c fascinated

2 Who is an archeologist?

a Auntie Rita's husband   b Auntie Rita   c Hunter's history teacher

3 What did Hunter do when he heard the name *Mérida*?

a He wondered about it.   b He ignored it.
c He went and talked to his mom and Auntie Rita immediately.

4 What did Hunter already know about Mérida?

a There was more than one place with the same name.
b It was always called Mérida.   c It was a small town.

5 What did Auntie Rita show him?

a a manuscript   b a secondary source   c a primary source

6 How did Hunter's mom feel when she heard him talking about history with Auntie Rita?

a bored   b angry   c surprised and happy

Reading Strategy: Evaluating

Evaluating is saying what we think about a text or a story. We say why we like it, what we learn from it, and what it makes us think about.

3 **Evaluate the story. Complete the review and give the story a star rating.**

Story Club

Review of the Story <u>A Place Called Mérida</u>   **Star Rating:**
By _____   ☆☆☆☆☆

Characters: How many? _____ What are their names? _____

Story Summary: _____ comes home from school and has dinner with his _____ . Then, he goes to do his _____ homework. He hears his mom talking to her friend, his _____ , on a video call. She lives in Mérida in _____ . He goes to talk to her, and she shows him a Roman _____ . They talk for an _____ ! It was his best _____ lesson ever!

What I Liked the Best: _____

What I Didn't Like: _____

What It Made Me Think About: _____

You should/shouldn't read this story because: _____

Grammar in Context

Modal Verbs of Deduction: *must*, *might*, and *can't*

When we are making guesses based on facts, we use modal verbs of deduction. When we're sure about something, we use *must*.

It **must** be the same place.

When we think something is possible, but we aren't sure, we use *might*.

It **might** be made of stone.

When we think something is not possible, we use *can't*.

It **can't** be the Mérida in Mexico.

1 **Match the sentences. Underline the modal verbs.**

1 It must be very hot outside.	a It isn't heavy enough.
2 She might like your present.	b The architecture is wrong.
3 He must be the new teacher.	c The temperature is 35 °C.
4 It might be a fresco from a Roman villa.	d He's carrying our science books.
5 That can't be a Roman building.	e I think she likes candles.
6 That ring can't be gold.	f The paint looks really old.

2 **Circle the correct modal verb.**

a The box **must / can't / might** be heavy because Jo can't lift it.

b The café **must / can't / might** be open. I think I saw a light inside, but I'm not sure.

c The phone call **must / can't / might** be from my mom because the number isn't her cell phone.

d This pendant **must / can't / might** be made of gold, but I'm not sure.

3 **How sure are you? Rewrite the sentences with *must*, *might*, or *can't*.**

a I'm sure Yana is happy about her test results.
   Yana must be very happy with her test results.

b Perhaps Yana is Russian.

_____

c Perhaps Yana has a pet cat.

_____

d I'm sure this isn't Yana's book. It has Alex's name in it.

_____

4 **You are a history detective! Look at the pictures and write sentences. Use *must*, *might*, or *can't*.**

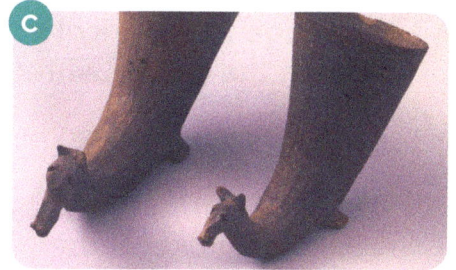

a

b

c

d

e

f

5 **Complete the text with the correct modal verbs.**

In 1545, the *Mary Rose*, a warship, sank off the south coast of England. Hundreds of years later, some fishermen were catching fish in the same area. Their nets caught on something underwater. "What are the nets caught on?" they wondered. "They [1]_____ be on rocks at the bottom of the ocean because the nets can't reach down there. The water is too deep."

Many more years passed, and in the 1970s, divers found something buried in the sand. "We think this [2]_____ be a warship, but we aren't sure yet," they said. Later, with carbon dating and other techniques, they said, "It [3]_____ be the *Mary Rose*. We're sure now! It [4]_____ be any other ship!"

6 **Look at the picture. What do you think it is? Write sentences.**

It can't be _____ because
_____ .

It might be _____ because
_____ .

It must be _____ because
_____ .

Values: Taking Care of Historical Monuments

1 How are historical monuments damaged? Look at the photograph. What do you think damaged this monument?

_____

2 Damage to historical monuments can have many causes. Match the causes with the effects.

Causes

1 Pollution from cars

2 Earthquakes cause

3 Space is needed for new buildings,

4 Tourists litter,

5 Visitors climb on monuments,

Effects

a so the appearance of monuments is spoiled for other visitors.

b so parts of the monuments are damaged.

c makes monuments look dirty.

d so monuments are demolished.

e monuments to fall down.

3 Which problem in Activity 2 is not caused by people? _____

4 Look again at the damage caused by people in Activity 2. What can we do to prevent that damage in the future?

_____

_____

5 Do you think we should take care of historical monuments? Who do you agree with the most? Mark ✓. Why?

a Monuments are an important part of our history. We have to protect them for future generations.

b Repairing historical monuments is very expensive. It's cheaper to build new buildings, so I think we should do that.

c I love old buildings and monuments. They're more beautiful than modern buildings!

d I don't like ancient monuments. I prefer modern architecture!

How Did I Do?

Check Your Oracy: Using Appropriate Body Movements and Gestures

1	I stood up straight and looked at the audience.	All the time / Most of the time / Sometimes
2	I used appropriate body movements.	All the time / Most of the time / Sometimes
3	I used the phrase on the cue card.	Yes / No

The Big Challenge

How can we research our family history?

a **What questions did you have about your family history?**

_____

b **Who did you interview?** _____

_____

c **How well did you do? Color the stars to score yourself.***

I prepared questions for my interview with my relative.	☆☆☆☆☆
I chose an object that told me more about my family history.	☆☆☆☆☆
I prepared and gave my presentation to the class.	☆☆☆☆☆
I maintained eye contact and used appropriate body movements and gestures while I was presenting.	☆☆☆☆☆

*(5 = Awesome! 4 = Pretty good, 3 = OK, 2 = Could be better, I = Needs more work!)

d **Which other presentation did you like the best?**

_____

e **What could you do better next time?**

_____

The Big Question and Me

Because of the things I have learned in this unit,

I will _____

_____

1 Look at the pictures. Write the words.

> detective   monument   tomb   document   archeological site   gold

a _____

b _____

c _____

d _____

e _____

f _____

2 Do the history quiz.

> carbon   column   foundations   Bronze   frescoes   villa   paleontologist

Quiz

1 Which age started around 2300 BCE in Europe? the _____ Age

2 What do you call someone who studies bones and fossils? a _____

3 What do you call something that supports a ceiling? a _____

4 What do you call the paintings on walls that you've learned about in this unit?

_____

5 What is another word for a big house with a big garden? a _____

6 What are under a house, but you can't see them? _____

3 Read and circle the correct words.

In Rome, the first [1]**aqueduct / villa**, the Aqua Appia, was built in 312 BCE to bring water to the city. [2]**Roman / Archeological** people used a lot of water. There were [3]**fountains / tiles** in the middle of squares with water, and there were public baths where people would go to relax. Roman roads were often [4]**straight / hidden** because armies needed to travel quickly. Sometimes roads were covered with [5]**cobblestones / horns**, which protected them. We know a lot about those times from [6]**secondary / grid sources**.

The Aqua Appia Today

4 **Rewrite these sentences using the past simple passive.**

    a They found the Rosetta Stone in 1799.

    _____

The Rosetta Stone

    b In 1939, they discovered an old ship at Sutton Hoo.

    _____

    c In 2018, our principal opened a new building at our school.

    _____

    d The team designed a very fast car last year.

    _____

    e They finished the exercises by lunchtime.

    _____

5 **Complete the sentences with the correct modal verb. Use *must*, *might*, or *can't*.**

    a I can't see very well, but I think that _____ be your friend Chung over there.

    b This pen isn't mine. It's blue, and mine is red. It _____ be Julia's because she's the only student in the class who has a blue pen.

    c That _____ be her brother because she only has a sister.

    d That coin _____ be from the Bronze Age—they didn't have coins back then!

    e This thumb print _____ be yours. Let's check! I'm not sure.

    f This _____ be my mother's favorite song. She listens to it at least ten times a day!

6 **Use the information in parentheses, and write sentences with non-defining relative clauses. Don't forget the commas.**

    a His daughter (acrobat) lives in Sydney.
       His daughter, who is an acrobat, lives in Sydney.

    b My grandmother (70 years old) plays tennis every day.

    _____

    c *Winnie the Pooh* (write / by A. A. Milne) is my favorite children's book.

    _____

    d The new phone (a huge memory) costs $250.

    _____

    e The historian (lived in Brasilia) hosted a TV show for children.

    _____

SPEAKING MISSION

1 **Match the words with the definitions.**

I	headphones	a	You hold this above your head when it's raining.
2	gloves	b	You need this when the battery in your phone, tablet, or laptop is low.
3	memory stick	c	An official document you need to leave or enter a country.
4	passport	d	You wear these on your hands when it's cold.
5	keys	e	A small folding case for carrying paper money and credit cards.
6	purse	f	You put this into your computer to copy and store information.
7	glasses	g	You need these to lock or unlock a door.
8	charger	h	A small bag that women carry their money, keys, and other small things in.
9	umbrella	i	You wear these in front of your eyes to help you see better.
10	wallet	j	You can put these over your ears when you want to listen to your music.

2 **Choose the correct phrases to complete the dialogue.**

> I'll call you if someone finds it   What does it look like   I lost my memory stick
> I'll get a form   Let me take your name and phone number   When did you lose it

Attendant	Good morning, this is the Middletown Lost and Found. How can I help you?
Girl	Yes, [1]_____.
Attendant	Just a minute. [2]_____. OK, so [3]_____?
Girl	I'm not sure. I had it at school yesterday, but I don't have it now.
Attendant	OK, so sometime in the last 24 hours. [4]_____?
Girl	It's a red plastic memory stick. It has my name on it.
Attendant	OK. [5]_____.
Girl	Sure. It's Joana Márquez. My phone number is 875-9693.
Attendant	OK, [6]_____.
Girl	Thank you very much.

Middletown Lost and Found

What can you remember about Unit 8? Do the quiz.

1. Historical clues can be objects, human and animal remains, or even whole
_____

2. Which country is the royal game of Ur from? _____

3. What is this? _____

_____

4. Who are historians and archeologists similar to?
_____

5. What were the names of the three girls in *The Metal Detector* story?
Julia, Cornelia, and
_____

6. Is there an *f* sound in the word *dough*? Circle the correct answer.   Yes / No

7. What do we call the story of a person's life?
_____

8. Complete the sentence.
The mask of Tutankhamun
_____ (discover) in 1925.

9. What's this?
I know! It _____ be a comb.

10. You lost your headphones. Complete the Lost and Found Attendant's question.
What _____ like?

Check your answers in the Student's Book. How did you do?
8–10 ☐ Wow!   6–7 ☐ Good job!   0–5 ☐ Try harder!

? 😃 How do we know what happened in the past? Write three things.

_____
_____
_____

9 Why does biodiversity matter?

1 ▶ 9.1 **Watch the video. Complete the graphic organizer.**

> protection   zebras   extinction   grasses   fungi   lions   reproduction   food

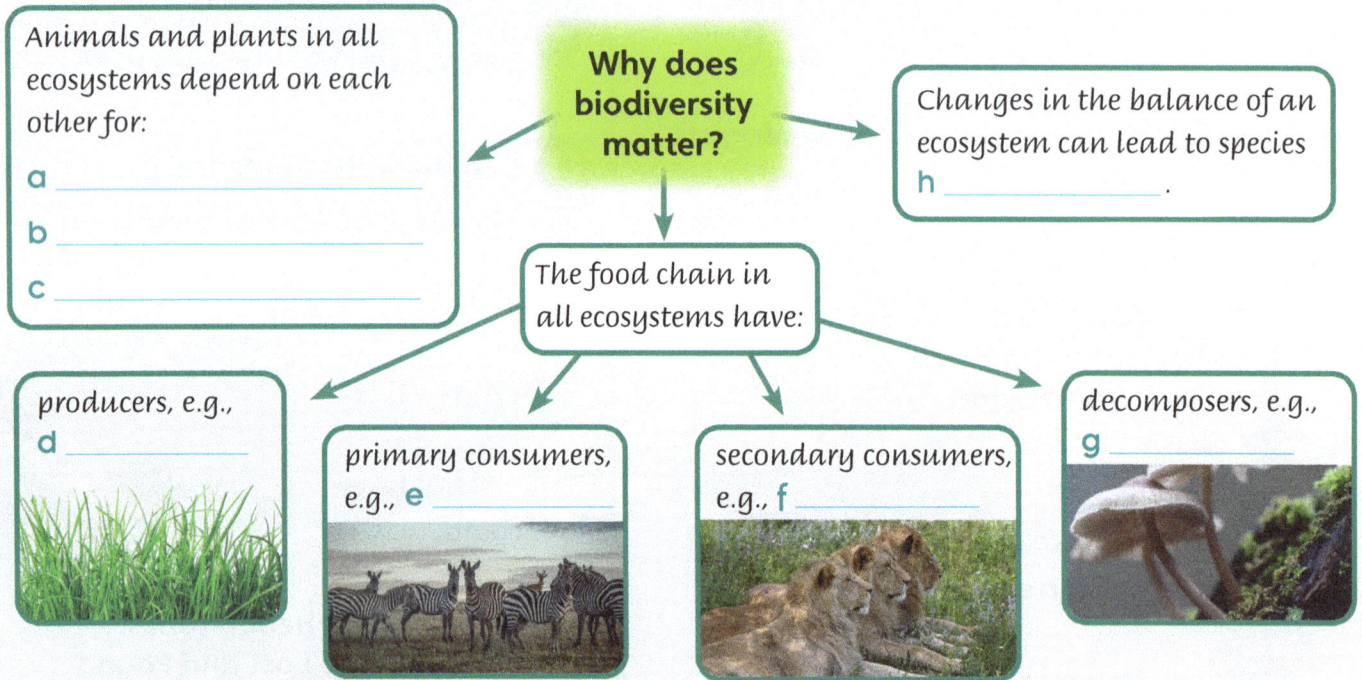

Animals and plants in all ecosystems depend on each other for:

a _____

b _____

c _____

Why does biodiversity matter?

Changes in the balance of an ecosystem can lead to species

h _____.

The food chain in all ecosystems have:

producers, e.g.,
d _____

primary consumers, e.g., e _____

secondary consumers, e.g., f _____

decomposers, e.g.,
g _____

2 Key Words 1 **Choose the correct words to complete the text.**

> interact   producers   decomposers   food chain
> biodiversity   fungi   ecosystem   consumers

We call the huge variety of animal and plant life in our world [1]_____. All animals and plants need each other to survive, and they also have to [2]_____ with air, sun, water, and soil. When living and non-living things exist together, it is called an [3]_____.

Everything in an ecosystem needs food. What eats what is called the [4]_____. It starts with [5]_____ like grasses and other green plants, which make their own food. Then, there are primary [6]_____, which eat plants, leaves, and grasses, and secondary consumers, which eat other animals.

Lastly, there are the [7]_____ like [8]_____, which turn dead plants and animals back into nutrients in the soil.

SB pages 182–83

Ready to Read: Nonfiction

1 | Key Words 2 | **Look at the pictures. Then, write the words.**

tentacle   snails   crab   algae

a _____ b _____ c _____ d _____

2 **Match the words with the pictures.**

1 carbon dioxide

2 filter

3 income

4 pipelines

3 **Choose the correct words from Activity 2 to complete the sentences.**

a Tourism near coral reefs provides many people with an _____ .

b Some animals _____ the water in the ocean and keep it clean.

c There are huge _____ on the ocean floor.

d In many parts of the world, there is too much _____ in the air, and this is causing global warming.

1 **Look at the photographs and read the interview. Choose the correct words to label the photographs.**

shell   tentacle   eye

All You Ever Wanted to Know About Snails

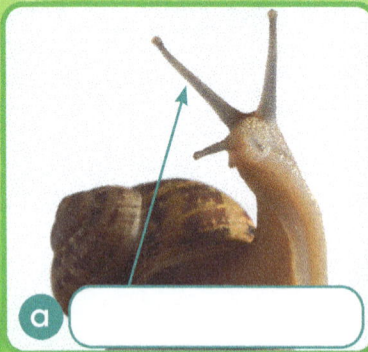

a

A Land Snail

b

A Freshwater Snail

c

A Marine Snail

What do you know about snails? I interviewed Jonathan Hedley-Smith, a malacologist, or snail expert, to find out more about these fascinating creatures.

Interviewer Could you tell our readers about all the different snails that live on Earth?

Jonathan I'll try, but there are literally thousands of different species of snails. They live on land, in freshwater rivers and lakes, and in the oceans. Snails that live in the oceans are called marine snails. Some snails are absolutely amazing, but others are so small and uninteresting, you hardly notice them!

Interviewer How do land snails fit into the food chain?

Jonathan They are primary and secondary consumers and decomposers. They eat living plants and invertebrates (animals that don't have a backbone), but they also eat dead plants and animals.

Interviewer Ah, now I understand why gardeners don't like land snails. They eat the plants in our yards.

Jonathan Yes, snails eat anything and everything! So if you grow flowers or vegetables in your yard, they are dinner for your snails!

Interviewer What can gardeners do to protect their plants?

Jonathan First of all, we should remember that snails are useful for their ecosystems, so we don't want to kill them all. We just want them to go somewhere else! However, if I had a big snail problem, I would try to protect my plants. I'd put crushed eggshells around them. Snails have very soft bodies, which the crushed eggshells can hurt, so snails won't go over them to reach the plants. You can also put coffee around your favorite plants because snails have an excellent sense of smell, and they hate the smell of coffee!

Interviewer Can you tell me something I don't know about snails?

Jonathan OK—do you know where their eyes are?

Interviewer Hmm, on their heads?

Jonathan Yes, but not exactly! Snails' eyes are on the ends of one of the pairs of tentacles on their heads, the longer pair. The shorter pair of tentacles helps snails to smell and to find their way around.

Interviewer I didn't know that! And a final snail thought?

Jonathan Snails are fascinating animals, and they aren't as slow as people think. Scientists have discovered that they can travel up to 1 meter per hour!

Interviewer Thank you!

Jonathan Hedley-Smith writes a weekly blog, Snail Thoughts.

Explore the Text

2 **Read the text again and answer the questions.**

a Where are snails found?

_____

b What is the role of land snails in the food chain?

_____

c Why do crushed eggshells stop snails from eating plants?

_____

d Why does coffee protect plants from snails?

_____

e Where are snails' eyes?

_____

Reading Strategy: Paraphrasing

When you read a text, it's a good idea to write it again in your own words. This is called paraphrasing. It's a useful way to check that you understand the text.

3 **Read this paraphrased sentence. Then, find and underline the sentence in the text that says the same thing.**

Snails won't go over crushed eggshells because they have soft bodies.

4 **Underline the important words in these sentences. Then, paraphrase the sentences. Remember to use your own words.**

a You can also put coffee around your favorite plants because snails have an excellent sense of smell, and they hate the smell of coffee!

_____

_____

_____

b Snails' eyes are on the ends of one of the pairs of tentacles on their heads, the longer pair. The shorter pair of tentacles helps snails to smell and to find their way around.

_____

_____

_____

The Second Conditional

We use the second conditional to describe things in the present or future that are hypothetical, unlikely, or impossible.

If I had a big snail problem, I would try to protect the plants.

If the producers died, there wouldn't be food for primary consumers.

We use the past simple in the *if* clause and *would/wouldn't* and the base form of the verb in the other clause. We sometimes use the contraction *'d* for *would*. We use a comma after the *if* clause if it is at the beginning of the sentence.

1 **Read the questions about the sentence in the grammar box and circle the correct answer.**

a   Does the speaker have a big snail problem?   Yes / No

b   Does the speaker know what to do about snail problems?   Yes / No

2 **Circle a or b to complete the sentences.**

1   If I had a test tomorrow,

   a   I didn't go to Jim's party tonight.

   b   I wouldn't go to Jim's party tonight.

2   If I received a text message in English,

   a   I have replied in English.

   b   I would reply in English.

3   If I saw some friends arguing in school,

   a   I would tell a teacher.

   b   I have told a teacher.

4   If I went to the U.S.A.,

   a   I would visit New York.

   b   I will visit New York.

5   If there were no more bees,

   a   many ecosystems would change.

   b   many ecosystems will change.

3 **Complete the sentences with the correct form of the verbs in parentheses.**

a   If we _____ (use) more solar energy, we _____ (produce) less carbon dioxide.

b   If fishermen _____ (not use) nets, other animals and fish _____ (not die).

c   If our rivers _____ (be) cleaner, more fish and animals _____ (survive) in them.

d   If we _____ (cut) down fewer trees, there _____ (be) more forests.

e   If there _____ (be) more forests, fewer species of plants and animals _____ (be) at risk of extinction.

4 **Put the words in order to make sentences.**

a give a presentation in class / I / primary consumers / I had to / would / If / talk about

_____

b swim / would / I / near the ocean / lived / I / If / every day

_____

c I / If / a samba show / go to / would / I / Rio de Janeiro / visited

_____

d would / more things / If / I / earlier / I / do / got up / before school

_____

e would / was / older / she / be able to drive / If / my sister / a car

_____

5 **What are the people *really* thinking? Complete the sentences using the words in parentheses.**

a If I __didn't have__ a lot of homework, I __would play__ soccer this evening. (not have) (play)

b If I _____ enough money, I _____ _____. (have) (buy / that phone)

c If I _____, I _____ _____. (run / faster) (win / the race).

d If I _____, I _____ _____. (be / taller) (be / good at basketball).

My Life

Complete the sentences so that they are true for you.

If I had to talk about an ecosystem, I _____.

If I went to a rainforest, I _____.

If I found some snails in my yard, I _____.

Spelling Patterns and Word Study

1 Look at the pictures and complete the words. They all have the same vowel sound.

a dinos _ _ _ r

b b _ _ _ _ _

c s _ _ _

d w _ _ _ k

2 Circle the letters that make the same vowel sound.

a claw   b author   c chalk   d draw   e small

Oracy

1 Which Oracy Time! topic did you and your partner give a talk about? Mark ✓.

⭐ Oracy Time!

how to use less plastic ☐

how to save water ☐

how to use less gasoline ☐

2 Did you structure your talk clearly? Did it have an introduction, organized points, and a conclusion? Circle the correct answer.

Yes / No

3 Which phrases from the cue cards did you use? _____

_____

Improve Your Writing

Although

Although is a connecting word. It means *in spite of something*. When we use *although*, we follow it with a subject and a verb.

Although I was really tired, I couldn't sleep.

I talked about saving water, although my plan was to talk about using less gasoline.

Remember to use a comma **after** the *although* clause if *although* comes first in the sentence. Use a comma **before** *although* if it comes at the beginning of the second clause in the sentence.

1 **Rewrite the sentences using *although*.**

a It was very early and very foggy, but Dad and I still went fishing.

b I know I have some homework, but I can't remember what the homework is!

c We made a lot of noise, but the baby didn't wake up.

d I missed your birthday yesterday, but I made you a card.

e My friend Sally didn't like the restaurant, but the food was delicious.

f There was a bus at 5 p.m., but Emily wanted to walk home.

2 **Circle the correct connecting word.**

a He lives in a very small apartment, **and / although / so** he is a millionaire.

b **Although / So / But** it was raining, we had a great time.

c My friend is quite small, **but / in addition / so** he can still run really fast.

d It is cold and snowy, **although / so / but** I plan to wear my heavy coat.

e I liked the food. **In addition / Therefore / However**, my friends didn't.

f My grandpa is visiting us soon. **So / Although / However**, we don't know exactly when.

Writing

1 **READ** Look at the flyer on page 191 in the Student's Book. Answer the questions.

a   Where do pygmy raccoons live? _____

b   What foods are bad for them? _____

c   Why are they endangered? _____

d   What should people do with their trash? _____

2 **PLAN** You are going to write a flyer about an endangered animal. Make notes in the graphic organizer.

Animal Name:	Picture of Animal

Where does it live?

How big is this animal and what does it look like?

What does this animal like to eat?

What's the problem?

What can we do?

3 **WRITE** Use your notes to write your flyer.

4 **EDIT** Read your work and mark ✓.

Did you:

- describe your animal and why it's endangered? ☐
- encourage your reader to take action? ☐

- give practical advice about what we can do? ☐
- include *although*? ☐

Ready to Read: Fiction

1 **Key Words 4** **Look at the pictures and write the words.**

gray falcon   lizard   coyote   plover   slug   whale   acorns   eagle   cricket

a _____
c _____
b _____
d _____
e _____
f _____
g _____
h _____
i _____

2 **Read and write the correct words.**

a   Plants that have narrow leaves and grow close to the ground.
   g _ _ _ _ _ _ _

b   Very small living things that sometimes cause disease. b _____

c   An African animal with one big horn in the middle of its forehead. r _____

1 Read the story and look at the photographs. Which two are dandelions? Mark ✓.

Homework

"What do you want to do first—math or English language arts?" Leo asked his cousin Charlie.

"Let's do language!" Charlie replied. "We have to read a poem and answer some questions. Thanks for helping me, Leo."

"I'm happy to help, Charlie. I love poetry," Leo said.

"I do, too," Charlie replied. "I really liked the poem about the plover and the crocodile that we read in school today, but I don't understand the one we have to read for homework."

"If we read the poem out loud, perhaps we'll understand it better," said Leo.

"OK, that's a good idea," Charlie answered.

They read the poem out loud, line by line.

O Dandelion

"O dandelion, yellow as gold,
What do you do all day?"
"I just wait here in the tall green grass
Till the children come to play."

"O dandelion, yellow as gold,
What do you do all night?"
"I wait and wait till the cool dews fall
And my hair grows long and white."

"And what do you do when your hair is white
And the children come to play?"
"They take me up in their dimpled hands
And blow my hair away!"

Then Charlie asked, "Do you know what a dandelion is, Leo?"

"No, I don't," said Leo. "But we need to find out. It's the first question."

> 1 What is a dandelion?
>   a) an animal b) a tree c) a flower
> 2 What is the dandelion's day like?
> 3 What does *dimpled* mean?

"Well, it can't be an animal because you can't blow an animal's hair away!" said Charlie.

"True. And a tree would be too big. So it's probably a flower. Yes, look! Here's a picture of a dandelion on my phone."

"Oh, I know what those are!" Charlie replied. "They grow in the grass in my grandpa's yard. OK, what's the next question?"

"What is the dandelion's day like?"

"Hmmm, boring! No, seriously, OK, this is cool. It's like the dandelion is a person waiting for children to come and play," said Charlie.

"Yes, that's called *personification*," Leo said. "It's when a plant or animal is represented as a person."

"Great. The next question is about … *dimpled*. I wonder what it means."

"It's something to do with hands," Leo suggested.

"I'll look it up," said Charlie. She got the dictionary and found the word. "Yes, *dimples are small hollow places in your skin*. I wonder if they are those hollow places where children's fingers join their hands."

"Yes, they must be," said Leo.

"Thanks a million, Leo. I understand the poem much better now," Charlie said.

SB pages 193–98

Reading Strategy: Understanding Poetry

Poems use imaginative language to talk about ideas. Sometimes they can be hard to understand, so here are some things that can help:

- Visualize the scene in your mind.
- Try to guess the meaning of the words from the context.
- Try to paraphrase the poem.

2 Read the story and circle the correct answers.

1 Why did Leo suggest they read the poem out loud?

    a to understand the poem better

    b to check the meaning of unknown words

2 How did they figure out the meaning of the word *dandelion*?

    a They guessed the meaning from the context.

    b They visualized the action.

3 Why did Leo look for a photo of a dandelion on his phone?

    a He didn't believe Charlie.

    b He wanted to check their idea.

4 What is *personification*?

    a a word used to describe flowers in poetry

    b when we talk about something as if it's a person

5 Which picture shows a *dimpled hand*?

a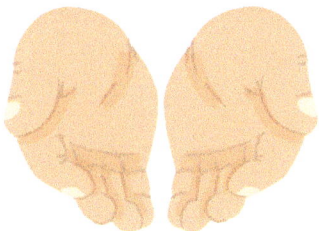

b

3 Paraphrase the first and last verses of the poem.

_____

_____

_____

_____

_____

_____

Grammar in Context

Embedded Questions

An embedded question is a question inside another question or statement. We often use them when we want to be polite. We use a question mark in embedded questions that start with *Can you tell me* and *Do you know*. We do not use a question mark after *I wonder*. Like reported questions, the order of the words is different from normal questions.

Do you know what a dandelion is? What **is** a dandelion?

I wonder if they are those hollow places where children's fingers join their hands.

Are they those hollow places where children's fingers join their hands?

1 **Write the words in the correct order to make embedded questions.**

a you / Can / live / you / where / me / tell

_____

b wonder / I / is / color / favorite / your / what

_____

c means / Do / know / *dimpled* / you / what

_____

2 **Complete the embedded questions.**

a Can _____ _____ _____ where gray falcons live?

b I _____ how many different species of bird there are in the world.

c Do _____ _____ how big an eagle is?

3 **Write embedded questions with these words. Add more words and make any other changes if necessary.**

a you / know / where / the Ecology Club / meet
<u>Do you know where the Ecology Club meets?</u>

b wonder / if / you / busy / tonight

_____

c you / know / where / eagles / live

_____

d you / tell / me / what / gray falcons / eat

_____

e wonder / if / your sister / have / homework / tonight

_____

174

SB page 199

4 Complete the embedded questions.

Girl ¹_____ _____ if you could help me.

Ranger Yes, of course.

Girl ²_____ _____ know where I can see bald eagles in the wild?

Ranger You can see them here and in every state of the U.S.A. except Hawaii.

Girl Oh, why not in Hawaii?

Ranger Well, the climate there is very different from the rest of the U.S.A.

Girl ³_____ _____ tell me what they eat?

Ranger Eagles eat mainly fish and small birds and animals. They also like eating meat from dead animals—what we call *carrion*.

5 Rewrite the questions in a polite form. Add a question mark if necessary.

a Where is our teacher?

Do you know _____

b Which poem do you like the best in this unit?

I wonder _____

c How many children are there in your school?

Can you tell me _____

My Life

Write three embedded questions to ask someone in your family who you don't know very well. Next time you see them, ask your questions. Then, write their answers.

I wonder _____

Can you tell me _____

Do you know _____

1 Look at the picture. How can we reduce our waste? Complete the table with the things we should do (Dos) and thing we shouldn't do (Don'ts).

Dos	Don'ts

2 What are the best ways to reduce waste? Number the boxes. I is the best. Then, write some of your own ideas.

a   Don't use plastic bags. ☐

b   Learn to repair things. ☐

c   Don't use disposable plastic plates and knives and forks. ☐

d   Eat everything on your plate. ☐

e   Learn the rules of recycling where you live. ☐

f   My ideas: _____

3 Choose one way to reduce waste and write about it here.

I'm going to _____

_____

I'm going to check this in _____ months' time.

How Did I Do?

Check Your Oracy: Structuring a Talk

1 My talk had a clear structure.	**Yes / No**
2 My audience understood my talk.	**All of it / Most of it / Some of it**
3 I used the phrases on the cue cards.	**All of them / Most of them / Some of them**

The Big Challenge   STEAM: Science

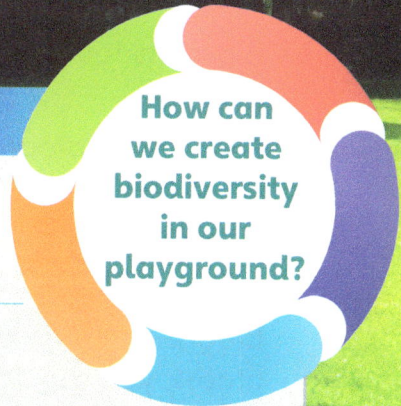

How can we create biodiversity in our playground?

a **Which insects and other animals did you want to attract to your playground?**

_____

b **How will your microhabitat attract them?**

_____

c **How well did you do? Color the stars to give yourself a score.***

I researched my ideas.	☆☆☆☆☆
I planned the microhabitat in the playground.	☆☆☆☆☆
I presented my plan to the class.	☆☆☆☆☆
I reflected on my classmates' feedback.	☆☆☆☆☆

*(5 = Awesome! 4 = Pretty good, 3 = OK, 2 = Could be better, 1 = Needs more work!)

d **Which of your classmates' ideas did you like the best?**

_____

e **What could you do better next time?**

_____

The Big Question and Me

Because of the things I have learned in this unit,

I will _____

_____

1 Choose the correct words to complete the crossword.

> bacteria predator species ecosystem
> filter producer consumer decomposer

Across

1 a group of animals or plants that share similar characteristics and can produce young animals or plants

4 It gets its food from dead plants and animals.

5 It eats food produced by plants and other animals.

6 When plants and animals exist together, they form an _____.

7 Before you drink the water in some places, you should _____ it.

8 These can cause diseases.

Down

2 It makes its own food.

3 An animal that kills and eats other animals is a _____.

2 Look at the pictures. Write the names of the animals.

a s _ _ _ _ _

b l _ _ _ _ _ _ _

c e _ _ _ _ _

d r _ _ _ _ _

e p _ _ _ _ _ _ _

f s _ _ _ _

3 Chose the correct word to complete the sentences.

> food chain millions pipelines biodiversity symbiotic

Today I'm going to talk about the world's oceans.
The ¹_____ of the oceans is amazing. ²_____
of different plants and animals live in them. There are many
examples of ³_____ relationships. That is when living things, animals and/or
plants, depend on each other to survive. In the oceans, we can also see how the
⁴_____ works, with the biggest fish at the top, of course! However, when
⁵_____ are built on the ocean floor, they can damage the ecosystem very badly.

4 **Complete the sentences using the second conditional.**

a If I _____ (have) enough money,
I _____ (travel) around the world.

b If I _____ (travel) around the world,
I _____ (visit) Australia.

c If I _____ (visit) Australia, I _____
(go) to the Great Barrier Reef.

d If I _____ (go) to the Great Barrier Reef,
I _____ (go) snorkeling.

e If I _____ (go) snorkeling, I _____ (see) amazing fish.

f If I _____ (do) that, I _____ (not / touch) the coral.

5 **Write these questions politely.**

a What time is it?

I wonder _____

b Where do you live?

Can you tell me _____

c How old is that boy?

Can you tell me _____

d Why are bees so important?

Do you know _____

6 **Rewrite these sentences using** *although*.

a I like peaches, but I prefer strawberries.

_____

b She has a bike, but she never rides it to school.

_____

c It looks like a dangerous shark, but it isn't.

_____

d She speaks a lot, but she doesn't always listen.

_____

e He loves going to musicals, but he doesn't go very often.

_____

f They have lots of books, but they haven't read all of them.

_____

1 **What were the five most important items your group chose for the time capsule?**

1 _____

2 _____

3 _____　　　　I think _____ is the most important of

4 _____　　　　all because _____.

5 _____

2 **Match the sentences with the parts of the talk.**

1　I'm going to talk about our time capsule.

2　The main point is that people in the future will see how we live now.

3　In conclusion, I think that people in the future will like our time capsule and find it interesting.

a　End of the Talk

b　Beginning of the Talk

c　Middle of the Talk

3 **Look at the pictures. What three things you should do during a presentation? Mark ✓.**

a

b

c

d

e　Can everyone hear me?

f　In conclusion...

What can you remember about Unit 9? Do the quiz.

1. **How big is the Pacific Remote Islands Marine National Monument, which you read about on page 184 in the Student's Book?**

   a 1 million square km

   b 1.2 million square km

   c 1.5 million square km

2. **Which ecosystem was the nonfiction text on pages 185 and 186 in the Student's Book about?**

   a coral reefs

   b rainforests

   c rivers and waterways

3. **Who called the crocodile?**

   _____

4. **How can we produce less carbon dioxide?**

   a By using more energy

   b By using more renewable energy

   c By using more water

5. **What animal was the flyer on page 191 in the Student's Book about?**

   _____

   _____

6. **Many coral reefs today are in**

   _____

7. **Complete the sentence using the verb in parentheses.**

   If I visited Los Angeles, I _____

   _____ (go) to Hollywood.

8. **You can't eat these fungi because they are** _____

9. **When might you use an embedded question?**

   a talking to your friend

   b talking to someone you don't know well

   c talking to your brother or sister

10. **What was the oracy skill for this unit?**

    _____

Check your answers in the Student's Book. How did you do?

8–10 ☐ Wow!   6–7 ☐ Good job!   0–5 ☐ Try harder!

? 😀 **Why does biodiversity matter?** Write three things.

_____

_____

_____

_____

All About Oracy!

Unit 1: Ground Rules

Ground rules help us understand how to behave when we are giving a presentation or having a discussion.

1 I think … because …

2 I agree because …

3 I disagree because …

Unit 2: Asking Probing Questions

We ask probing questions to find out more information or to get more detailed answers from someone.

4 What do you think about …?

5 How?

6 Why?

Unit 3: Active Listening

An active listener makes eye contact and responds to show they are interested in what someone is saying.

7 That's interesting.

8 I see.

9 That's a good idea.

Unit 4: Expressing Points of View

When we express our point of view, we give reasons to support it. We also give reasons when we agree or disagree with someone else's point of view.

In my opinion, *Star Wars* is the best movie ever …

I agree because …

2 I agree because …

3 I disagree because …

10 In my opinion, …

Unit 5: Giving Encouragement

When we listen to other people's ideas, we can give encouragement by sounding interested and making positive comments.

11 That's a great idea!

12 That sounds like fun.

13 That's a good point!

Unit 6: Confident Use of Evidence to Support an Argument

When we argue for or against something, we use evidence to support what we are saying. This evidence might be things from our own experience or things we have learned or heard about.

What do you think ... ?

2 I agree because …

3 I disagree because …

14 I know because …

15 For example, …

Unit 7: Projecting Your Voice

When you give a presentation, it's important to project your voice confidently so that everyone can hear you. Check with your audience and speak more loudly if necessary.

16 Can you hear me now?

17 Can you speak up?

18 How's this?

Note: "Can you speak up?" is a way that someone in the audience can encourage a speaker to project their voice.

Unit 8: Appropriate Body Movements and Gestures

Pay attention to your body movements and gestures. Stand up straight and look at your audience when you speak.

19 Let me tell you about …

Unit 9: Structuring a Talk

We can help people understand what we are saying by making sure our talks are clearly structured. Provide an introduction, organized points, and a conclusion.

20 We're going to talk about …

21 The main point is …

22 Also, …

23 In addition, …

24 In conclusion, …

Acknowledgments

The authors and publishers acknowledge the following sources of copyright material and are grateful for the permissions granted. While every effort has been made, it has not always been possible to identify the sources of all the material used, or to trace all copyright holders. If any omissions are brought to our notice, we will be happy to include the appropriate acknowledgments on reprinting and in the next update to the digital edition, as applicable.

Key: U = Unit.

Photography

All the photos are sourced from Getty Images except the following.

UI: Courtesy of Deepika Kurup; **U8:** Courtesy of Sylvia Gummery.

Illustration

Antonio Cuesta; Diana Santos; Diego Diaz; Emanuella Mannello; Jimena Sanchez; Monica Auriemma; Robert Dunn.

Cover illustration by Mónica Armino (Advocate).

Typesetter

Blooberry Design and QBS Learning.